The Power of God's Grace

The Final Solution

EVANGELIST FRANCIS BOAFO

WESTBOW
PRESS®
A DIVISION OF THOMAS NELSON
& ZONDERVAN

This book is a work of non-fiction. Unless otherwise noted, the author and the publisher make no explicit guarantees as to the accuracy of the information contained in this book and in some cases, names of people and places have been altered to protect their privacy.

WestBow Press books may be ordered through booksellers or by contacting:

WestBow Press
A Division of Thomas Nelson & Zondervan
1663 Liberty Drive
Bloomington, IN 47403
www.westbowpress.com
1 (866) 928-1240

ISBN: 978-1-5127-7244-9 (sc)
ISBN: 978-1-5127-7245-6 (hc)
ISBN: 978-1-5127-7243-2 (e)

Library of Congress Control Number: 2017900927

Print information available on the last page.

WestBow Press rev. date: 05/10/2017

Contents

Acknowledgments

I give glory to the Lord Jesus Christ, by whom the Spirit of God, provided me the grace to receive what you are about to, read in this book, "**The Power of God's Grace:** *The Final Solution.*" He enabled the eyes of my heart, and the spirit of my mind to receive His thoughts, and to understand what He is saying to His people in these day and age. His name alone deserves praise forever. Amen! I have written this book to all people, especially Christians, who want to overcome, as Jesus wants us to in this life and the age in which we live.

Forward

Missionary Boafo's new book distinguishes itself, notably, from his earlier books. The theme of his previous book, 'our identity in Him', posed a challenge that was more, easily apprehended than 'the power of God's grace' working within each of us. The present challenge is best, represented in his arresting phrase 'subject to the kingdom of self'. The false kingdom of self is a deceptive illusion all are subject to except for the power of God's grace. The insidious nature of such delusion is that it different, by definition, for every individual. Accordingly, that which you need to overcome daily is 'the kingdom of self'.

Because of Missionary Boafo acknowledges he has written this book to all people, it must be approached, individually, in the context of each person's particular need, allowing God's thoughts expressed in His Eternal Word to be quickened to each spirit and heart, as it was received and presented here. This book must be seen as a resource to 'wrap our hearts around', as it ministers to the need of the moment in our lives. — **Pastor Mark Estes**

Introduction

Praise God who is love. The Grace of God represents His love story for humanity. God's love is from everlasting to everlasting. He has shown you His love through the sacrifice of Jesus Christ, His Holy Son, who came into the world with abundance of God's grace. Through Jesus Christ, God has provided all you need to triumph in this corrupt world. By His grace, God has provided you with all spiritual blessings in the heavenly places and everything that pertains to your life and godliness.

Through Jesus Christ, God has made provision to produce a champion out of your life. He has provided His Word to save you, and His wisdom and power to help you overcome ungodliness and worldly lusts. This is the grace of God to you. Therefore, the grace of God is here through Jesus Christ, to help you avoid indulging yourself in the very things that diminish the status of the people of the world, in relation to God's expectations for man. God wants you to overcome in the face of evil, lawlessness, and corruption in this age. In all issues pertaining to your life, you will reign and overcome because you have received abundance of grace, and the gift of righteousness from the One Man, Jesus Christ.

There is grace that Jesus provides you and grace that you seek, if you are serious about your Christian life. By the power of the grace in Jesus Christ, God enabled the prophets to write the mysteries of the things to come, many hundreds of years ahead of their fulfillment. Because of the grace of God, you live a victorious Christian life, pleasing God in your ways.

The grace of God appeared to humanity as God's unmerited favor until Jesus came on the world scene. After the advent of Jesus Christ, the full thrust of the grace of God came to humanity, which has become both unmerited favor to redeem man and to deliver creation from the bondage of decay. Today, the grace of God is here to sustain and empower you to live a victorious Christian life. The Spirit of grace, the

Holy Spirit, teaches you to deny ungodliness and worldly lust and to live soberly, righteously, and godly through all of your life's issues.

If you are in Jesus Christ, you are in grace and have the power of the Word, the power of wisdom, and the power of God to overcome the corruption that influences many in this world. Therefore, through the grace of God, you grow consistently in your ability to define your life issues, including your ministry, by the Word of God, truth, all in righteousness. This is an act of obedience, which activates the power of the presence of Father and Son with you and within you.

God knows the daily difficulties you face in life, and He knows where you are failing. In your difficulties, God calls on you to come boldly to the throne of Grace to receive mercy and find grace to help you. You cannot continue to fail God since He has opened the door to the throne of Grace to you. You cannot continue to use grace as an excuse to indulge yourself just as the world does.

Concerning grace, Apostle Paul said, "Should you continue in sin that grace may abound?" His answer is, certainly not! If you died to sin through your baptism, how can you live any longer in sin? In your baptism, death occurred and your new self came into being. Through Jesus Christ, God provides the grace you need, but you must seek His help so you would overcome life's challenges, which would otherwise produce unfaithfulness to your Redeemer.

LESSON: *One of the reasons many fail God and live unfaithful lives to Christ is the lack of knowledge of their identity in Christ Jesus and of God's provisions for an overcoming life through the power of grace. In addition, many do not understand the fear of the Lord.*

The next time you tell anyone you are in grace, there must be evidence that after redemption, you are progressively overcoming ungodliness and worldly lusts. The Spirit of grace is daily teaching you to live righteously and godly, because you know, and are aware of the soon-coming Savior, Jesus Christ. Today, God does not want you to fall short of entering into His divine goodness, His rest. Since the grace of God has appeared to all men, it represents God's final solution to help humanity orient herself to God's demand for heaven.—**Evangelist Francis Boafo**

Chapter 1

Discovering the Grace of God

——Part 1——

Through Jesus Christ, the grace of God has come to humanity. God was pleased to invest all His fullness bodily in Jesus. The Bible says Jesus is the image of the invisible God, the firstborn of all creation. Through Him God created all things that are in heaven and that are on the earth, visible and invisible. Whether thrones or dominions or principalities or powers. God created all things through Him and for Him. The Bible says in Revelation 3:14, "These things say the Amen, the Faithful, and True Witness, the Beginning of the creation of God".

The Amen, the Faithful Witness, refers to Jesus, who became the Christ, the Lamb of God, slain for our sins before the foundation of the world. The heavenly host said the following about Jesus your Savior: "Worthy is the Lamb who was slain, to receive power and riches and wisdom, and strength and honor and glory and blessing!"

Apostle John said he heard every creature in heaven, and on earth, under the earth, in the sea, and all who are in them, saying, "Worthy is the Lamb who was slain to receive power and riches and wisdom, and strength and honor and glory and blessing!" (Revelation 5:12).

The Bible says to you in Colossians 2:10, "And you are complete in Him, who is head of all principality and power".

LESSON: *You are complete in Jesus. Therefore, do not allow the world to define who you are by its system. You are a child of the King of the whole universe and blessed with all the spiritual blessings in the heavenly places.*

However, if you fail to know your status in Christ Jesus, you may live as though the world owes you something. Consequently, you could seek after your needs from the world when God says to you that He will supply all your needs, according to His riches in glory by Christ Jesus.

God raised Jesus from the dead, seated Him at His right hand in the heavenly places, far above all principalities and power and might and dominions, and every name that are named, not only in this age, but also in that which is to come. God has put all things under Jesus' feet.

Again, because of Jesus' humility and taking on Himself the cross, God exalted Him and gave Him a name that is above all names. Every knee should bow to Him, of things in heaven, on earth, and under the earth. Soon, every tongue will confess that Jesus is Lord.

Jesus represents the power of God, which is above all principality and power. He said to the high priest of His day, "You will see the Son of Man seated at the right hand of power and coming on the clouds of Heaven." Currently, Jesus is positioned with His Father on His throne, at His right hand.

You are complete in Jesus because in Him, you have received the circumcision of your heart, and God has put off your body of sin. Spiritually, God buried you with Jesus through your baptism. He raised you with Jesus through your faith. These benefits come to you by the hand of God who loves you and wants to fill you with all His spiritual resources, even His fullness (Ephesians 3:19). The requirement for God's fullness in you is that you establish yourself in the following:

- Grow your life of faith, which is obedience to God's Word—an indication Christ dwells in you. If you are in Christ, you share His character, which is a life of obedience to the Word of God that you are knowledgeable. If there is something you do not know the Holy Spirit, speaks to your spirit the need to obey Jesus in your life circumstances. He never fails to speak to you if you will listen.
- Grow, and become established and rooted in the life of love. Love for God and for people is always an act of obedience to God's commands or to His Word to you.
- Grow your knowledge of Christ's love for you and, for that matter, for all people. If you acknowledge the love of Christ,

you will come to an understanding that God saved you to live for Jesus and not for yourself.

Grace as the Unmerited Favor of God

Through Jesus, humanity receives freedom from bondage to sin and corruption. Understand that the lifestyle of sin and corruption, are the product of the law of sin and death. Understand also, that the grace of God has been around since the beginning of human history.

God showed His grace when He made coats of skins to clothe Adam and Eve in the Garden of Eden, after they lost God's glory. God showed His grace when He saved righteous Noah and his household from the flood that deluged the whole earth. God showed His grace, when He saved Lot and his family before He destroyed Sodom and Gomorrah. God showed His grace, when He fed rebellious Israel with manna and quail in the wilderness.

God showed His grace, when He prepared food for the prophet Elijah in the wilderness, during his flight from Jezebel. God showed His grace when Christ gave you gifts of His Spirit to serve in His church. God shows His grace each day by waking you up after a good night's sleep. The enemy of your status in Christ, and his agents wish they could destroy you while you sleep, but the power of Jesus protects you.

God showed His grace when Christ died to enforce the atonement for the sins of all humanity. The Bible says in Romans 5:6, "For when we were still without strength, in due time Christ died for the ungodly." Again, God made you alive with Jesus. Though you were dead in your trespasses, He forgave you, and nailed to the cross of Jesus, all the requirements that stood against you.

With the advent of Jesus Christ, the grace of God became not only God's unmerited favor, but also the power, the wisdom, and the Word of God. This grace is available to help you and all humanity live strong in your redeemed life. The grace of God is here to help you do the will of God in your life circumstances, and to triumph in this ungodly and lustful world.

The Fullness of the Grace of God Revealed

God revealed His Word, His wisdom, and His power to humanity as the grace of God, which came through Jesus Christ. In John 1:17, the Bible says, "For the law was given through Moses, but grace and truth came through Jesus Christ". Jesus came into the world full of the grace of God, and of His fullness, we have all received grace for grace.

LESSON: *The grace of God is not a static status that you arrive at only to remain stagnant. You need grace for every area of your life because the grace of God comes to you with the power of the Holy Spirit, the Spirit of Grace, to help you overcome your daily challenges.*

There is grace given to you by Jesus, and grace you seek to help you handle multiple life issues so you would learn to avoid lawlessness. You may confront daily issues that could draw you into the path of lawlessness. Other times, you may face challenges that could draw your heart to pursue evils of this world. This makes it critical to seek the grace of God.

What then is the grace of God, since the grace of God has appeared to all people? Even though it has appeared to all, it is a requirement that people receive it, to initiate salvation in their lives. If you claim to have received the grace of God or you are in a period of grace, you are declaring the following:

1. You have received Jesus Christ as your Savior. You have received salvation through the Word of God preached to you. In addition, you have come into newness of life, and you have a new lordship over your life, the lordship of Jesus Christ.
2. You have received the wisdom of God, the power of God, and the Word of God to refuse or deny ungodliness, and worldly lust in your life. Ungodliness and worldliness plague many in this world.
3. You have received the Word of God, the wisdom of God, and the power of God to live righteously, soberly, and godly in the present age. Does it mean you will never act in unrighteous

ways ever? Not at all, but you have to ensure your deeds are not intentionally motivated to do evil.

4. You have received the Word of God, the wisdom of God, and the power of God to help you live in obedience to Jesus your Lord in every circumstance. You did not only receive Jesus as your savior, but He must also be your Lord, whom you must learn to obey.

5. You have received the Word of God, the wisdom of God, and the power of God to assist you in whatever Christ has called you to do. Because of the grace of God, you do all you do in life and ministry in righteousness, holiness, godliness, and truth, all in the fear of the Lord. You repent for deviations. (Refer also to Titus 2:11–14).

The Spirit of grace will help you live with the awareness of the soon-coming Savior, Jesus Christ. The Spirit of grace also helps you stay awake, with the awareness that Jesus shed His blood to redeem you from every lawless deed, and purified you for Himself to become part of His own special people, who are zealous for good works.

Therefore, it is not a light thing to claim to have the grace of God or to be under grace. There must be evidence of the fruit of the power of grace in your life—that the grace of God is helping you change your life to God's pleasure.

Do not let anyone talk you out of your belief in the Gospel of Jesus Christ. It is your spiritual and physical manual for the journey to the kingdom of heaven. The Word, the wisdom, and the power of God are available to you through Jesus Christ, your Lord and Savior. God, therefore, expects you to be successful in doing all He expects out of your saved life.

Apostle Peter encourages you to be even more diligent to make your calling and election sure, for if you do what the Apostle commands, you will never stumble. However, you have to grow your faith and knowledge of God from the pages of the Bible, which the Holy Spirit directs you, daily. Jesus gives you the wisdom to know His Father, even understand the Holy Spirit.

Jesus is the grace of God revealed to humanity and creation. Jesus is the Word, the wisdom, and the power of God. Therefore, I am going to consider the aspects of the Word, the wisdom, and the power of God, which are resident in Jesus. This will help you understand why the grace of God is His final solution to help humanity overcome inconsistent lifestyles that deviates from the life He expects all people to live.

LESSON: *Understand this that for everything God demands from your Christian life, you will need to find the grace of God to fulfill to His pleasure. You cannot do God's will apart from the grace of God and for that reason, Jesus said to you, "…Apart from me you can do nothing".*

Chapter 2
Discovering the Grace of God

—— Part 2 ——

Jesus, the Living Word of God

God created the universe by His Word so that the things that are seen today came into being from things that were invisible. I will consider the part that His wisdom played in creation later in this chapter.

The Bible says in John 1:1-4, "In the beginning was the Word, and the Word was with God, and the Word was God. He was in the beginning with God. All things were made **through** Him, and without Him nothing was made that was made. In Him was life, and the life was the light of men." This is so because God created all things by His Word, wisdom, power, and understanding, which represent Jesus.

The psalmist said in Chapter 138 verse 2, "I will worship toward your holy temple, and praise your name for your loving-kindness and your truth; for you have magnified your word above all your name". God has magnified, or exalted, His Word above all His name.

The Bible says in Hebrews 4:12-13, "For the Word of God is living and powerful, and sharper than any two-edged sword, piercing even to the division of soul and spirit, and of joints and marrow, and is a discerner of the thoughts and intents of the heart. And there is no creature hidden from His sight, but all things are naked and open to the eyes of Him with whom we must give account."

The Word of God is powerful, and has the ability to discern every hidden thing in your soul and spirit. It is able to go deep into the source of your life, the marrow. The Bible says life is in the blood (Leviticus

17:11), and the marrow is the source of your blood. The Living Word is able to discern every thought, and intent of your heart.

Therefore, Jesus—the Word of God—has the ability to discern all aspects of the known, and hidden issues in your life. Nothing in your life escapes His scrutiny. All things are naked and open to His eyes. This, therefore, calls for openness, whenever you approach Jesus—openness because you cannot hide your sins in His presence. He knows all your ways and where your heart lives.

LESSON: *Before you utter a word before Jesus, He knows everything about you. Because He knows all about you, and He loves you, do not allow the devil to trick you with fear to live unfaithful to Jesus, your redeemer.*

The Word as Light

In addition to the Living Word of God being powerful and sharper than any two-edged sword, the Word of God is also light, the true light, which gives light to every person who comes into the world. Unfortunately, when people come into the world, they pursue ways that corrupt their lives. Corruption opens up a way for darkness to come into your life, which gains the upper hand if you fail to deal with it. It opens you up to give way to worldly lifestyles, behaviors, and mindsets, making it possible for the introduction of blemishes in your life all over again.

The Bible says in Ecclesiastic 7:29, "Truly, this only I have found: That God made man upright, but they have sought out many schemes". Fortunately, the light of God's Word, Jesus Christ, outshines the darkness of this world, and the darkness cannot overcome it. The light of God's Word leads you to the cross of Christ, where you receive the unmerited favor of God's salvation. After salvation, learn to stay in the light of God's Word. The power of the Word of God saves you because you responded correctly to the Word of the grace of God.

In your recreated life, God's Word wants to lighten your ways and bring life to you. King David said in Psalms 119:105, "Your Word is a lamp to my feet and a light to my path," and in Psalms 119:11, "Your Word have I hidden in my heart, that I might not sin against you".

Because you are a new creation in Christ, learn to hide the Word of God in your heart. It will direct your path in this world of darkness.

God's Grace in Human Form

When Jesus came into the world, He said, "Sacrifice and offering you did not desire, but you have prepared a body for Me. In burnt offerings and sacrifices for sin, you have had no pleasure. Then I said, Lo, I come (in the volume of the Book it is written of Me) to do Your will, O God" (Hebrews 10:5-9). When He said, "Sacrifice and offering, and burnt offerings and offering for sin You did not desire, neither did You have pleasure in them" (which are offered according to the law), and, "Lo, I come to do Your will, O God," He takes away the first so that He may establish the second.

God's will for Jesus was that He lay down His life, and His body as a sacrifice for the sins of humanity, to redeem them. Jesus said in John 10:17-18, "Therefore, my Father loves me, because I lay down my life that I may take it again. No one takes it from me, but I lay it down of myself. I have the power to lay it down, and I have the power to take it again. This command I have received from my Father".

The Word of God, which is active and powerful, and through whom God created all things in the heavens, and on the earth, became flesh and lived among us as Jesus Christ. God prepared a body for His Word, Jesus, "...A body you have prepared for me". He came into the world as the light, the love, the truth, the way to God, and the grace of God; to redeem and save humanity from bondage to sin and to free creation from its bondage to corruption.

The Bible says, "For God so loved the world, that He gave His only begotten Son, that whoever believes in Him should not perish but have everlasting life." When Jesus came into the world, He said, "As long as I am in the world, I am the light of the world", because the Word was light. He said this just before He healed the eyes of a blind man. The light of God's Word still shines in this dark world. God does not want you to perish but have everlasting life; but He needs your cooperation in your life issues to help guide you.

LESSON: *To do the will of God is to learn to obey the Word of God—written or which comes to you from the Holy Spirit. The Holy Spirit works in you to help you do God's will.*

The Word of God and You

Note that in the Word of God you will find the mercy, the compassion, the promises, and the love of God. This is how you will know that God has good intentions for your life in Christ Jesus. If the love of God for humanity made Him give up His only son to help anyone who believes in Him, and promises that you should not perish, then you must be convinced of His love for you who lives through Jesus Christ. If God's love made Him give up His only Son, will He not graciously give you all things with Christ?

The faith that makes you stand strong in this life comes from your knowledge of the Word of God. Consequently, handle the Word of God more seriously each day. You will learn to become like the seed in Jesus' parable, which fell in good soil. As you become knowledgeable in the Word of God, handle it in the following ways:

1. Commit verses to memory so your heart will learn to keep them.
2. Treasure the instructions it provides you.
3. Make your heart attentive to the wisdom it provides.
4. Through prayer, call out for insight.
5. If you do not understand, the Word received, raise your voice in prayer, and ask for understanding.
6. Seek the Word of God as you would seek money in this world.
7. Search for the Word of God as you would a hidden treasure hid from you.

LESSON: *Always remember that the Lord knows exactly your attitude towards His Word and He wants you to be more diligent.*

The Spirit of Grace, the Holy Spirit, will instruct you in the ways you should go. He uses the Word of God to do so. Therefore, take heed to the command in Colossians 3:16 to "Let the Word of Christ dwell in you richly in all wisdom, teaching and admonishing one another in psalms, and hymns and spiritual songs, singing with grace in your hearts to the Lord".

Your diligence in handling the Word of God will open you up for your steady transformation into the image of Jesus Christ, God's Son. This is so because the Word of God grows your faith, which helps your obedience to Jesus.

So then, faith comes by hearing, and hearing by the word of God. Note that God has given the scripture through men, inspired by the Holy Spirit, and is profitable for doctrine, for reproof, for correction, for instruction in righteousness: That the man of God may be perfect, thoroughly furnished unto all good work.

The Word of God is required to help you fulfill the following:

1. Grows and shapes your belief system to help your knowledge in Christ and the principles required for your Christian living and victories.
2. Bring correction and admonishment to your Christian walk and ways. It helps you grow in the knowledge of Christ and provides the wisdom you need for salvation through faith.
3. Give direction to your Christian life so you can live along the path of righteousness, which the Holy Spirit leads you in, daily.
4. Grow you in the power of God, enabling you to live in this world without corrupting or influenced by the world.
5. Grow your soul, spirit, and body in righteousness, holiness, and godliness, to fashion you for all good works.
6. Grow you up into salvation.

Some Benefits of God's Word

It is important that you seek the Word of God as you would money in the world. Reference Proverbs 2:1-13. In addition, search for the Word as you would a hidden treasure.

The following are some of the benefits you gain from the Word of God:

- It gives you wisdom for life and for your Christian life.
- It gives you knowledge and understanding for living.
- It teaches you to understand the fear of the Lord.
- It guides your paths in the way of justice in your life issues.
- It teaches you to understand righteousness in your life issues.
- It delivers you from the way of evil and men of perverted speech, who forsake the paths of righteousness to walk in falsehood (darkness).

Wisdom cries out to you, to treasure the Word of God because in it, you will find the wisdom and the power you need to triumph in the situations that confronts you. In the fear of the Lord, He gives you knowledge and understanding. The Word of God provides you with the understanding and conviction that none of the things happening in your life will destroy you.

LESSON: *Your life is on God's watch, and He will not allow anything in your life to destroy you.*

God says to you in 1 Corinthians 10:13, "No temptation has overtaken you except such as is common to man; but God is faithful, who will not allow you be tempted beyond what you are able, but with the temptation will also make the way of escape, that you may be able to bear it." Therefore, in your seasons of difficulties or temptations, listen to Jesus because the Holy Spirit will, without fail, instruct you in the ways you should go—a way of escape to help you through your situations.

Pursue the Way of Grace

Many things could happen in your life, but do not let the magnitude of life's difficulties or problems intimidate you to hurry yourself ahead of God's work in your life. After you have identified the Word of God, which address your situation, quiet your heart and mind until you receive wisdom to know what God wants you to do to overcome your situation. This is how you apply the grace of God in your life—the Word to give knowledge, wisdom to know what God wants you to do, and power to overcome in your situations.

Your God is faithful from everlasting to everlasting. That is why He commands you to not be anxious about anything; but in everything, by prayer and supplication with thanksgiving, let your request known to Him. He will guard your heart and mind with peace that is beyond understanding through Christ Jesus.

LESSON: *Your God is very faithful! He is true to His word and promises to you. He will never fail you when you depend on His promises. He always keeps His covenant with His people.*

Jesus, the Wisdom of God

The Bible wants you to encourage yourself in heart, walk in love with your fellow men, and to have full assurance of understanding and to the knowledge of God the Father and of Jesus Christ. Why do you need to encourage yourself? This is so because all the treasures of wisdom and knowledge abide in your Lord, Jesus Christ. The Bible says Jesus is the wisdom of God, and by His wisdom, God established the world, and by His understanding stretched out the heavens.

In our natural world, wisdom is the ability to use knowledge in productive ways. To use knowledge productively, you must have the insight, the understanding, the perception, and the intelligence about the available knowledge you have. Jesus is the Amen, the Faithful and True Witness, and the beginning of the creation of God. Wisdom was the beginning of the creation of God. In teaching about the wisdom of God, the Bible says in Proverbs 8:22-31,

"The Lord possessed me at the beginning of His way, Before His works of old. I have been established from everlasting, From the beginning, before there was ever an earth. When there were no depths I was brought forth, when there were no fountains abounding with water. Before the mountains were settled, before the hills, I was brought forth;

While as yet He had not made the earth or the fields, Or the primal dust of the world. When He prepared the heavens, I was there",

"When He drew a circle on the face of the deep, When He established the clouds above, When He strengthened the fountains of the deep, When He assigned to the sea its limits, So that the waters would not transgress His command, When He marked out the foundations of the earth, Then I was beside Him as a master craftsman; And I was daily His delight, rejoicing always before Him, Rejoicing in His inhabited world, And my delight was with the sons of men". Jesus' delight was in the sons of men!

Because Jesus was from the beginning of all things, He said to the Jews, "Most assuredly, I say to you, before Abraham was, I AM". Because the Jews lacked the spiritual understanding of what Jesus said, His statement caused Him problems. The Jews attempted to stone Him. He hid Himself from them and went out of the temple.

Just as in Jesus' experience with the Jews, do not be afraid to give to people the insights the Holy Spirit has taught you. There are people who want to learn. Always be generous to teach others what the Holy Spirit has taught you.

In His prayer to the Father, Jesus said in John 17:4-5, "I have glorified you on the earth. I have finished the work, which you have given me to do. And now O Father, glorify me together with yourself, with the glory which I had with you before the world was." Jesus was the Word and wisdom of God who had glory with the Father from the beginning.

The Word and Wisdom from the Beginning

You must learn to acknowledge the mysterious nature of the God, the One you cannot see but serve through faith. As referenced in John 1:1, in the beginning, the Word was with God. Likewise, wisdom was from the beginning with God, "The Lord possessed me in the beginning of His way, before the earth was, Before His works of old". This is so because Jesus represents the Word and wisdom of God, who was in the beginning with God.

How appropriate! Jesus, the Word and the wisdom of God, was in the beginning with God as a Master Craftsman; "And I was daily His delight".

God created all things through His Word, His wisdom, and through His power, Jesus, who became the Christ. God anointed Him, and sent Him to us in a human form to redeem humanity who had lost the glory of God. In the days when He was in a mortal body, Jesus went to the synagogue in His hometown. He received the book of the prophet Isaiah, opened, and found the place as recorded in Isaiah 61:1-3,

"The Spirit of the Lord GOD is upon me, because the Lord has anointed me to preach good tidings to the poor; He has sent me to heal the brokenhearted, to proclaim liberty to the captives, and the opening of the prison to those who are bound; to proclaim the acceptable year of the Lord, and the day of vengeance of our God; to comfort all who mourn; to console those who mourn in Zion, to give them beauty for ashes, the oil of gladness instead of mourning, the garment of praise for the spirit of heaviness; that they may be called trees of righteousness, the planting of the Lord, that He may be glorified".

The Word and the wisdom of God came among humanity with God's anointing, and power to do the following:

- Preach good tidings to you.
- Heal your broken heart.
- Proclaim liberty to your areas of captivity.
- Open your spiritual prison to set you free in areas where you are bound.
- Proclaim that the acceptable year of the Lord is now.
- Proclaim the day of vengeance of God.
- To comfort and console you who have come to Him, but mourn.
- To give you beauty for your ashes, and oil of gladness for your seasons of mourning.
- To provide a garment of praise for your spirit of heaviness.

He does all these for you so the world and the spiritual realm will see you as a tree of righteousness, a person God has planted. This brings glory to God.

Jesus demonstrated the power of God in every circumstance of His life. As indicated in Proverbs 8, Jesus, the Wisdom of God, has a special delight for the sons of men. No wonder He chose to die for humanity so His Father would forgive our sins.

Chapter 3
Discovering the Grace of God

—— Part 3 ——

Jesus, the Power of God

As I indicated earlier, all the fullness of the Godhead dwells in Jesus bodily, and for that reason, He is the head of all principality and power. Therefore, the name Jesus is powerful beyond all principality and power in the whole universe except His Father who was pleased that His fullness should dwell in Jesus. Through Jesus and His sacrifice on the cross, all things are being reconciled to God, things on the earth and in heaven, making peace through the blood of His cross. Everything about Jesus is power!

Apostle Paul said to the believers in Romans 1:16, "For I am not ashamed of the gospel, for it is the power of God for salvation to everyone who believes, to the Jew first and also to the Greek". Therefore, Jesus is not only the Word (as we usually know of Him) and the wisdom of God, but He is also the power of God. The word of His gospel will save completely, those who depend on Him through obedience of faith in His gospel.

The Bible says in Jeremiah 10:12, "He has made the earth by His power; He has established the world by His wisdom, and has stretched out the heavens by His discretion".

Very early in my Christian life, when I began chasing after God with all my heart, the Holy Spirit inspired me to understand that God first created what He needed to create all other things—the earth, the heavens, and all creation. This knowledge did not mean anything to me then, but I kept it in my heart.

Today, as I go through these passages in Colossians, Proverbs, and other passages in the Bible, it has become clearer to me the awesome abilities of your and my God. With your God, all things are possible. He created what He needed to create all things in heaven, on the earth, and under the earth. You can raise your chest, walk, and live with confidence that your God is able and He is with you through the power of the Spirit of grace. Through Jesus Christ, his power, wisdom, and His Word have come to strengthen you to overcome in this life.

Demonstration of Power

In the natural, anyone who has power demonstrates that power through manifestations. I watched two young men at a gym try to show each other they have power in their muscles. I watched carefully, with interest. They added discs of weights to a lift apparatus, and each lifted the apparatus in turns. They kept adding the 25 lb. discs of weights and each tried to lift the apparatus. With the increasing weights, it got to a point where one of the young men came to his limit. He could not lift the apparatus any longer.

Unlike the two young men showing the power in their muscles, in the spiritual realm, power, is not demonstrated by physical means but spiritual. The power of the name of Jesus, which all things bow to, is not physical. While He was present in His physical form, Jesus demonstrated His spiritual power. His power transcends natural and spiritual powers.

The Bible says in 2 Corinthians 10:4-5, "For the weapons of our warfare are not carnal, but mighty through God to the pulling down of strongholds, casting down arguments and every high thing that exalts itself against the knowledge of God, bringing every thought into captivity to the obedience of Christ."

In the place called Gethsemane, Judas came with a band of officers from the chief priests and Pharisees to arrest Jesus. They came with lanterns, torches, and weapons. Jesus, knowing all things that were coming upon Him, went out and said to them, ""Whom are you seeking?" They answered Him, "Jesus of Nazareth". Jesus said to them, "I am He." When He said this, they all drew back and fell to the ground" (John 18:3-6).

The power of Jesus radiates out of His life, because of His holy and righteous living. The fight of the end time will be a fight on the platform of righteousness and holiness against the spirits of darkness.

Jesus and His saints will war, based on their brightness of holiness and righteousness. No power of darkness will be able to withstand the brightness of Jesus' and His saints' glory. This power comes from their righteous and holy living. This is one of the reasons God commands you to practice the attributes of your new nature in Christ Jesus. The attributes of your new nature in Christ include righteousness, holiness, and godliness. Because the Holy Spirit is in you, God expects you to walk in truth as well.

LESSON: *Do not take God's command to put on the attributes of your new nature in Christ lightly. If you fail to obey His command, you cannot become a part of the warriors with Jesus.*

Unlike Adam, Jesus did not corrupt His life at any time through disobedience to God His Father. His holy and righteous lifestyle makes everything bow to Him. He was "...Declared the Son of God with power according to the Spirit of holiness ..." (Romans 1:4).

Living among us, Jesus performed great and unmatched miracles, which God enabled Him to do. "...The works that I do in My Father's name, they bear witness of Me". Again, Jesus said in John 14:10-11, "Do you not believe that I am in the Father and the Father is in me? The words that I say to you I do not speak on my own authority, but the Father who dwells in me does his works. Believe me that I am in the Father and the Father is in me, or else believe me for the sake of the works themselves."

LESSON: *Just as His Father worked through Him, Jesus wants to work through you because you are in Him and you live through Him. Therefore, learn to orient your heart, to obey the word of God, just like Jesus towards His Father.*

Jesus changed water into wine, opened blind eyes, raised the dead, calmed the sea, and walked on the sea. When people stricken by leprosy came to Him, they went away cleansed. The Bible says in John 21:25, "And there are also many other things that Jesus did, which if they were written one by one, I suppose that even the world itself could not contain the books that would be written." Therefore, Jesus did many miracles, which the season He was living in could not capture all.

Jesus cast out a mute demon from a man. When the mute demon came out, the man spoke clearly. Some of the people said Jesus cast out the demon by Beelzebub, the prince of demons. That was very interesting indeed! Answering them, Jesus said, "Any kingdom divided against it self is brought to desolation, and a house divided against a house falls".

Then Jesus said something very powerful in Luke 11:20-22, "But if it is by the finger of God that I cast out demons, then the kingdom of God has come upon you. When a strong man, fully armed, guards his own palace, his goods are safe; but when one stronger than he attacks him and overcomes him, he takes away his armor in which he trusted and divides his spoils."

Jesus is the stronger one and He came from God to destroy the works of Satan, with which he has captivated humanity, "He who sins is of the devil, for the devil has sinned from the beginning. For this purpose the Son of God was manifested, that He might destroy the works of the devil" (1John 3:8). The 'finger of God', as stated in Luke 11, is the power of God, whom Jesus represents. Therefore, He said to them, a stronger than Satan, Jesus Christ, has come to overcome and destroy him, and to take away his armor by which he has kept humanity in the prison of disobedience to God. Apart from Jesus, you can do nothing against the power of evil and Satan in this world.

LESSON: *Ensure to pray against division and selfish ambitions in your home. If you fail to do so, it could grow into all kinds of vile practices, creating a platform for Satan to operate in your home.*

LESSON: *The only power in the whole universe that overcomes Satan is the power of God in Christ Jesus. His name Jesus possesses everything from God to protect you from Satan and from evil.*

In the Holy Scriptures, God promised beforehand through His prophets, the coming of His Son, His word, wisdom, and power, Jesus Christ.

LESSON: *In the spiritual realm, holiness, godliness, and righteousness represent power. This is why God has blessed your new nature with these attributes, and He commands you to practice them in your life issues.*

The practice of holiness in your life activates God's power in your life and ministry. A greater measure of God's presence comes over you for any ministry Christ has assigned to you, because you love righteousness and holy living. The presence of Jesus in your life comes with His power. With the power of Jesus' presence, you overcome every form of evil and evil enticements that could draw you into disobedience against your loving Jesus.

Since you have received redemption, by the shed blood of Jesus, He represents your life, and you have to learn to live through Him and for Him. If you do, He will always come to you with His overwhelming power—the power of grace to help you overcome in this age of lawlessness. His presence with you begins at the point of your sincere life of obedience—obedience to His Word and the Word the Holy Spirit presents to you.

The Way to God, the Father

The presence of Jesus in your life is also an indication of the presence of the Father. The reason for this happening in your life is your obedience to His Word, including the Word the Holy Spirit quickens in your heart in the midst of your life issues. Jesus walked in total obedience to His Father; hence, the presence of the Father was very powerful in His life. You learn to put down self, and allow God's Word to take precedence in your life. You cannot live any other way except through Jesus, because He is the Way, the Truth, and the Life, and no one comes to God the Father except by Him.

Power in the Name of Jesus

The name of Jesus carries awesome power. God has highly exalted Jesus above all. His name is so powerful at the mention of the name Jesus, every knee bows, of things in heaven, and things in earth, and things under the earth. Every tongue should confess that Jesus Christ is Lord, to the glory of God the Father (Philippians 2:9-11).

The Bible says in Acts 10:38, "How God anointed Jesus of Nazareth with the Holy Spirit and with power, who went about doing good and healing all who were oppressed by the devil, for God was with Him". The Bible encourages you to continue in your life of obedience. You do so not because a pastor, a deacon, or a Christian Brother or Sister is looking over your shoulder.

LESSON: *Just as God anointed Jesus with the Holy Spirit and with power, Jesus likewise wants to anoint you with the Holy Spirit and with power.*

- **The Name of Jesus—the Power for Salvation**

The Bible says in Acts 4:11-12, "This Jesus is the stone which was rejected by you builders, which has become the chief cornerstone. And there is salvation in no other One; for there is no other name under heaven given among men by which we must be saved."

- **Baptism in the Name of Jesus and the Holy Spirit**

On the day of Pentecost, when the Holy Spirit descended on the believers, Apostle Peter preached to the crowd who responded to the sounds of tongues. He said to them, "Repent and be baptized every one of you in the name of Jesus Christ for the forgiveness of your sins, and you will receive the gift of the Holy Spirit. For the promise is for you and for your children and for all who are far off, everyone whom the Lord our God calls to himself".

Apostle Paul met some disciples and he asked them, "Did you receive the Holy Spirit when you believed?" They said, "No, we have not even heard that there is a Holy Spirit." Apostle Paul baptized them in the name of the Lord Jesus and when he laid his hands on them, the Holy Spirit came on them and they began speaking in tongues and prophesied (Acts 19:2-6).

In Acts 10, the Holy Spirit revealed to Cornelius, a centurion to go to Joppa to go call Apostle Peter. When Peter came to Cornelius' home, he testified to his household about Jesus. The Bible says while Apostle Peter testified about Jesus, the Holy Spirit fell on all who heard the Word. Therefore, he baptized them in the name of Jesus.

• The Name of Jesus—the Power for Healing

The authorities arrested Apostle Peter and John because they healed a lame man in the name of Jesus. The Sanhedrin questioned them and their response is recorded in Acts 4:10, "Let it be known to you all, and to all the people of Israel, that by the name of Jesus Christ of Nazareth, whom you crucified, whom God raised from the dead, by Him this man stands here before you whole."

A man, who was lame from birth, positioned at the gate to the temple, called the Beautiful. They placed him there to ask alms of those entering the temple. He asked to receive alms from Apostle Peter and John, who were about to go into the temple. Apostle Peter said to the lame man, "I have no silver and gold, but what I do have I give to you. In the name of Jesus Christ of Nazareth, rise up and walk!" Immediately his feet and ankles became strong, and he leaped up, stood, and began to walk and entered the temple with them, walking and leaping and praising God (Act 3:2-8).

• The Name of Jesus—the Power for Deliverance

In the city of Thyatira, Apostle Paul and Silas were going to prayer. A slave girl possessed with the spirit of divination followed them saying, "These men are the servants of the Most High God, who proclaim to us the way of salvation". She did this for many days until Apostle Paul, distressed by her actions, cast out the spirit with the name of Jesus Christ. The spirit came out that very hour.

The Power of the Blood of Jesus

Jesus is the head of His Church, His body. He is the beginning, the first-born from the dead, that He may be pre-eminent in all things. By the power of the blood of Jesus, it pleased the Father to reconcile all things to Himself through Jesus. This includes things in heaven and things on the earth, making peace with the Father through the blood of His cross.

Through the power of the blood of Jesus, your alienation from God has ended. You are no longer an enemy of God in your mind, pursuing wicked works. Through the blood of Jesus, you are reconciled to God, and have become a child of God. Now, the goal of Jesus is to present you holy, without blemish, and without any fault to the Father. Therefore, He encourages you to continue in your faith, grounded and settled, and not moved away from the hope of the Gospel. Make the hope of the Gospel your daily delight.

To many intellectuals of our day, the Gospel you claim to love and trust is foolishness. To them, it is foolish to claim salvation by the God you do not see, trusting and depending on Him for a glorious future. I met a man at our neighborhood mailbox, and I asked if he were a Christian. He said to me, "Why do you ask, because I am not going to tell you?"

LESSON: *To have Jesus and not be proud of belonging to Him is an indication that the devil still has you deceived.*

I said to the man, "For the events that are going to come upon the whole world, you will be glad you were a Christian and living for Jesus." He responded, "I know all about that, and this is the fear Christians have, and therefore are forced to believe." Wow!

The Bible says in Romans 1:22, "Professing to be wise, they became fools". The God you serve and trust is well alive, and what the world considers as foolishness about His Gospel, you trust and proclaim is the power of God, which is Jesus Christ. What the world considers as foolish is wiser than men, and what the world considers as weakness about your God is stronger than men.

The Blood of Jesus and Redemption

The Bible says in Ephesians 1:6-7, "To the praise of the glory of His grace, by which He has made us accepted in the Beloved. In Him we have redemption through His blood, the forgiveness of sins, according to the riches of His grace."

Your Redemption is here and now

Concerning redemption, the Bible says in Leviticus 25:25-28, "If one of your brethren has become poor, and has sold his property, and if any of his relatives comes to redeem it, then he shall redeem that which his brother sold. And if the man has no redeemer, and, he himself is able to redeem it, and he has enough for its redemption; then let him count the years of the sale of it, and restore the remainder to the man to whom he sold it, that he may return to his possession. But if he is not able to have it restored to himself, then what was sold shall remain in the hand of him who bought it until the year of jubilee. And in the jubilee it shall be released, and he shall return to his possession."

My friend today is your day of redemption and restoration. The blood of Jesus has paid for it all, including your redemption and your restoration. You do not have to wait for the year of jubilee nor wait for a full year. Today is your year of jubilee and today is your full year. Jesus is ready to redeem and restore whatever you allowed the devil to take possession from you.

LESSON: *Oftentimes, the devil gain advantage and takes possession of your "goods"— spiritual or physical—for your carelessness in some areas of your life.*

Jesus came to set you free in every area of your captivity. You can receive your redemption and restoration today. Jesus is able to restore and reset your life and possessions today, if you believe.

The Blood of Jesus and Cleansing

The Bible says in 1 John 1:6-9, "If we say we have fellowship with Him, and walk in darkness, we lie and do not practice the truth. But if we walk in the light as He is in the light, we have fellowship with one another, and the blood of Jesus his Son cleanses us from all sin. If we say we have no sin, we deceive ourselves, and the truth is not in us. If we confess our sins, He is faithful and just to forgive us our sins and to cleanse us from all unrighteousness."

LESSON: *For you as a believer, the blood of Jesus cleanses you because you acknowledge your wrongdoing and sin. If you do, then, the blood of Jesus is ready to cleanse you from all sin.*

Never say to yourself that because Jesus knows about your sin, His blood will take care of it. You have to confess your known sins and not wait on Jesus to do it for you. The Bible says if you confess your sins, God is faithful and just to forgive your sins. This is an everlasting covenant enacted through the blood of Jesus, which works for you as long as you live in this body. God wants to help you do all through Jesus Christ, to His pleasure. He also wants you to live through Jesus Christ, because in Him you find grace to do everything in life with righteousness and purity of heart.

The Blood of Jesus and Blood on Doorpost

Just before the deliverance of the children of Israel from the land of Ancient Egypt, God said to Moses in Exodus 12:12-13, "For I will pass through the land of Egypt this night, and will smite all the first-born in the land of Egypt, both man and beast. And I will execute judgments against all the gods of Egypt. I am Jehovah. And the blood shall be a sign to you upon the houses where you are. And when I see the blood, I will pass over you. And the plague shall not be upon you for destruction when I smite in the land of Egypt."

Jesus is the mediator of the new covenant, and His sprinkled blood not only delivers, but speaks better words for you than the blood of

Abel. Remember, the blood of Abel cried to God from the ground after his brother Cain murdered him. The blood of Jesus is your covering against the wicked in this world and against their plots.

The blood of Jesus is a covering over you because you live a submitted life to Him. Therefore, no weapon formed against you shall prosper. Consequently, any and every tongue raised against you in judgment will not succeed. This is a heritage for you as the servant of the Lord, because your righteousness is from the Lord.

Chapter 4

Jesus Christ—the Grace of God for Humanity

The Bible says in John 1:14, "And the Word became flesh, and dwelt among us, and we beheld His glory, the glory as of the only begotten of the Father, full of grace and truth." Jesus came to His own people but His own people did not receive Him. However, all who did receive Him, and those who believe in His name, He gave them the right to become the children of God. These are those born of God and no man initiated or had a hand in this phenomenon.

Apostle Paul said in 1 Corinthians 2:7-8, "But we speak the wisdom of God in a mystery, which God ordained before the ages for our glory, which none of the rulers of this age knew; for had they known, they would not have crucified the Lord of glory." However, unlike the rulers of this age, you know Jesus Christ through the power of His grace. He wants to give you wisdom to know Him deeper. He wants you to understand the mysteries of the kingdom of heaven.

This is the reason you are growing in your diligent pursuit of the grace of God. Because you know the mysteries of the kingdom of heaven, you diligently seek for everything that comes with your knowledge of the kingdom of heaven. You seek Jesus in order to help you triumph in your life issues to God's pleasure.

The Status of Adam at Creation

God created Adam next to God; in the likeness of God, He created Adam. The Bible says in Psalms 8:4-6, "What is man that You are mindful of him, And the son of man that You visit him? For you have made him a little lower than the angels, and you have crowned him with glory and honor." In fact, the Hebrews law uses the word Elohim in place of angels. God said, "Let Us make man in our image, according to our likeness" (Genesis 1:26).

In John 10:31, the Jews took up stones again to stone Jesus. He said to them, "Many good works have I shown you from my Father. For which of those works do you stone me?" The Jews answered Him, saying, "For a good work we do not stone you, but for blasphemy, and because you, being a man, make yourself God." Jesus answered them in John 10:34, "Is it not written in your law, I said, you are gods?" David also said in Psalm 82:6, quoting from the law, "I said, you are gods, and all of you are children of the Most High".

Therefore, God created man, a little lower than Him, and crowned him with glory and honor. In verse 6 of Psalm 8, it reads, "You have made him to have dominion over the works of your hands; you have put all things under his feet". Unfortunately, when Adam and Eve yielded to Satan's deception and his lies, they disobeyed God, and man lost his position and the glory of God.

Now we see not yet all things put under man. "But we see Jesus, who was made a little lower than the angels for the suffering of death, crowned with glory and honor; that He, by the grace of God, might taste death for everyone" (Hebrews 2:9).

Praise God for Jesus

You can praise God for Jesus Christ. By Him and through the grace in Him, you receive salvation through faith in the Word of His Gospel. It is not of yourself, but the gift of God's unmerited favor, lest you should boast. By Jesus, you have become a new creation. In your new creation, God expects you not to live like the Adam generation—in rebellion. Your new creation is of the generation of the Last Adam, Jesus Christ, who is a life-giving spirit. God is creating a new generation from the Last Adam who will obey Him (Romans 8:29).

Through Jesus Christ, God has given you His Word, His wisdom, and His power to help restore you to your place and the glory Adam lost. All who are born again are candidates of this new creation and the generation of the Last Adam. Your new position is with Christ in the Most High God, at His right hand. God has hidden you with Christ in God Himself. That is your current position and you have to acknowledge this as true, so you would orient your life to walk in the power that comes with it. Let this be the delight of your soul.

Can you believe you are at the right hand of the Most High God, where Jesus sits? The Bible says this about you— that you are now the child of God and the glory about you is not yet revealed; but when Jesus returns, you shall be like Him. This calls for a life of purity as stated in 1 John 3:3. God has restored you to your place, the place that Adam lost. However, you have to understand, and know the demand your new status places on you, in God's divine order in Jesus Christ. Your new creation makes you a candidate for greatness in heaven. God has blessed you with every spiritual blessing in the heavenly places in Christ.

LESSON: *The many failures of some of the redeemed are because of an inability to use all that God has provided in Jesus Christ, His Son.*

LESSON: *Know your current state in Jesus Christ so you will not yield your life to carelessness, lacking focus of whom God is making you. Rather, be diligent and live like a soon-coming king who is in training, a champion of the living God.*

Note that God left Adam for Satan to tempt him. To Satan, it was temptation for evil, but to God, it was a test of obedience for promotion and greatness. Satan also tempted Jesus with evil, but unlike Adam, He remained faithful to His God and Father. God, therefore, promoted and perfected Him to become the source of eternal salvation to all who obey Him (Hebrews 5:8-9).

Like Adam and Jesus, your life could be in your spiritual "Eden" or "wilderness". You are undergoing testing to prove the genuineness of your faith. The outcome will be your promotion to greatness. The Bible says in 1 Peter 1:6-7, "In this you greatly rejoice, though now for a little while, if need be, you have been grieved by various trials, that the genuineness of your faith, being much more precious than gold that perishes, though it is tested by fire, may be found to praise, honor, and glory at the revelation of Jesus Christ". The knowledge that God is testing the genuineness of your faith will make the grace of God very attractive to your soul.

The Lifestyle of Jesus and You

The lifestyle of Jesus is an example He has set before you to follow. The Bible says in Colossians 2:6-7, "As you therefore have received Christ Jesus the Lord, so walk in Him, rooted and built up in Him and established in the faith, as you have been taught, abounding in it with thanksgiving". Jesus said in John 14:12, "Most assuredly, I say to you, he who believes in Me, the works that I do he will do also, and greater works than these he will do, because I go to My Father." What He did includes His lifestyle and functions.

LESSON: *The reason many fail in their pursuit of Jesus is, they are not rooted and built up in Him. Moreover, they fail to frequent the throne of grace to find the strength they need to overcome. You have to establish yourself in Jesus for a consistent lifestyle as He did. Learn to live with thanksgiving for Jesus Christ, who strengthens you with His grace.*

If you are rooted and built up in Jesus, you will overcome every form of deception that ensnares many in this world because in Him, you find grace to help. Jesus knows you will be tempted just as He and Adam were tempted. The devil tempts you to prove to God you are unfaithful and not worthy of His goodness towards you.

The devil always forgets that you did not deserve any of God's goodness, but He gave Jesus to die to save you. The Bible says, "What then shall we say to these things? If God is for us, who can be against us? He who did not spare His own Son, but delivered Him up for us all, how shall He not with Him freely give us all things?" (Romans 8:31-32)

On the other hand, the greater reason the devil tempts you, is to see if you would be careless and ignorant for him to steal the things you have gained in Christ. God tests you to fulfill His covenant of blessings in your life—promotion to your greatness. Jesus was never careless; therefore, He did not give the devil opportunity to steal anything from Him.

LESSON: *Understand that no one attains to greatness in God's system without any form of testing.*

So learn from Jesus, who is your example. He knows God and His love for Him! Nevertheless, the Bible says in Hebrews 5:8-9, "Though He was a son, yet He learned obedience by the things which He suffered. And having been perfected, He became the author of eternal salvation to all who obey Him." Seek grace for your life issues so you will not live to please self, your self-image, or your ego; instead of seeking to please the Lord.

The life of Jesus is your example. He was selfless! He did only those things that pleased God, His Father. Therefore, He was not "**subject to the kingdom of self**".

Remember the life of Joseph in Ancient Egypt. Before the promise of greatness happened, the Bible says the word of promise tested him (Psalms 105:18-19). Note that it was not Jesus' idea to go to the wilderness. The Spirit of God led Him there to go through temptation at the hand of the devil. The devil tempted Jesus with many ideas, expecting he could catch Jesus in one point of unfaithfulness to His Father God.

Nevertheless, the devil failed because Jesus knew His identity in regards to His relationship with God His Father. Jesus loves you. He feels for the weaknesses in your life and He desires that you will seek the grace in Him to help you live a faithful life to God through Him.

The Bible says in Hebrews 4:15, "For we do not have a high priest who is unable to sympathize with our weaknesses, but one who in every respect has been tempted as we are, yet without sin". Therefore, Jesus knows the strategies that can sustain your life and He knows you could fail if you confront life challenges by yourself. He calls on you to seek Him and the grace in Him to help you, even in your time of need.

The Person of Jesus and You

As stated in John 1, Colossians 1, and 1 Corinthians 1, Jesus is the Word, the wisdom, and the power of God. He was in the beginning with

God. He is the image of the invisible God the firstborn of all creation (Colossians 1:15). That means the Word of God and the wisdom of God, Jesus Christ, were God's first creation. In the fulfillment of times, God clothed His Word, His wisdom, with a human body and He came into the world with power as the Last Adam.

Jesus came to Earth clothed in a human body but without the gene of Adam. The Bible says, "The first man Adam became a living being. The Last Adam became a life-giving spirit". God is in the process of creating a new generation of humans through Jesus Christ. This is what I have referred to in my book, "Re-Created for Greatness", as the "Jesus Generation".

The Jesus Generation

The "Jesus Generation" includes the people of Revelation 12:11. If you are a part of the Jesus generation, and have the Spirit of Christ, you learn obedience to Jesus and the Father. In fact, your delight is to do the will of the Father at all tines, irrespective of the pain that sometimes accompanies doing so. Jesus makes grace available to you to help you in your life of obedience.

Jesus healed the paralytic man and said to him in Mark 2:11, "I say to you, rise, pick up your bed, and go home". The paralytic man rose up, immediately picked up his bed, and went out before them all. They were all amazed and glorified God, saying, "We never saw anything like this!" In other words, what was impossible had now become possible through Jesus Christ before their very eyes.

LESSON: *What was impossible in your life must become possible for people to see His glory, and to know that you belong to Jesus.*

Creation acknowledges Jesus Christ as the Lord of lords and the King of kings. As God's favored part of creation that He has wonderfully made, you have to learn to acknowledge Jesus not only as your savior but also as Lord in your daily life choices, decisions, and lifestyles. Lords demand obedience to their commands and rules.

LESSON: *Jesus must not just become your savior but also the Lord, whom you must learn to obey. This is how you will attain to your eternal salvation (Hebrews 5:9).*

Through obedience to His Father, Jesus received perfection and became the source of your eternal salvation. It should be your inner desire to learn to obey Jesus—obedience to His command (His Word) and His voice through the Holy Spirit, which comes to you in your daily life issues.

Jesus has Grace for you

Jesus came to the earth full of the grace of God. Therefore, He overcame all forms of human depravities and lived a submitted and obedient life to God His Father. This grace has appeared to all men, to save people who believe the Gospel of Jesus Christ. The person saved by the grace of God will need more daily grace to help live a victorious Christian life in this corrupt and evil world.

The grace of God through Jesus Christ will help you live in the light of your new creation. The light of your new creation is Jesus Christ, which means you can live no other way but through Him. In many of Apostle Paul's letters to the churches, he would begin by saying, "Grace and peace to you." Apostle Peter would similarly write, "Grace and peace be multiplied to you".

Since the heavenly call progresses from one degree of glory to another, Jesus wants you to seek His grace to help you step by step as you journey along these glory paths. Jesus provides you with enough grace to help you to your next level of glory. Therefore, learn not misuse the grace Jesus provides you. The Bible says in 2 Corinthians 3:18, "But we all, with unveiled face, beholding as in a mirror the glory of the Lord, are being transformed into the same image from one degree of glory to another, just as by the Spirit of the Lord."

Now the righteousness of God has been manifested apart from the law, although the law and the Prophets bear witness to it—the righteousness of God through faith in Jesus Christ, to all who believe.

For there is no difference; for all have sinned and fall short of the glory of God, being justified freely by His grace through the redemption that is in Christ Jesus, whom God set forth as a propitiation by His blood, through faith, to demonstrate His righteousness, because in His forbearance God had passed over the sins that were previously committed, to demonstrate at the present time His righteousness, that He might be just and the justifier of the one who has faith in Jesus.

From the above passage, God, by His grace through Jesus Christ has done the following for you:

1. You now know the righteousness of God that comes to you apart from the law, but by your faith. Jesus is the righteousness of God to humanity. In Jesus, you become a new creation.
2. By the grace of God in Jesus, God has passed over your former sins. This reveals God's righteousness in justifying you by your faith in Jesus.
3. You are justified by the grace of God as a gift, through the redemption that is in Jesus Christ. Because God has done this for you and for all humanity through Jesus Christ, if any fails to put their faith in Jesus, God will be just and righteous in imposing the consequences. Through Jesus, God has done all He will do to help you and humankind to live by faith in Jesus Christ.
4. God put forward Jesus as a propitiation for your sins by His blood, which you must receive by faith.

The blood of Jesus is available to wash away your sins as you journey towards your eternal destiny. However, you have to avoid willful sinning.

LESSON: *Willful sin is to hear the voice of the Word of God and the voice of His Holy Spirit speaking to you to do what honors God, but you ignore them all to pursue what pleases self.*

Through Jesus Christ, God has given you everything that pertains to life and godliness. Everything means exactly that—everything; everything you will ever need to make it to heaven. These include all spiritual blessings in the heavenly places. God does not want you to fail in your quest for the kingdom of heaven. He will be justified if anyone fails to use His grace to deny ungodliness and worldly lust.

Jesus, the Revealer of His Father

Jesus said in Matthew 11:27, "All things have been delivered unto Me by My Father, and no one knows the Son except the Father. Nor does anyone know the Father except the Son, and the one to whom the Son wills to reveal Him." You can make yourself a candidate for Jesus to reveal the Father to you. And in John, "No one has seen God at any time. The only begotten Son, who is in the bosom of the Father, He has declared Him."

LESSON: *The many double-standard Christian expressions among God's people reveal that many do not truly know the Father or the Son. Do not let church attendance or the pursuit of a ministry become the satisfying drive of your heart. Seek God the Father and Son.*

Jesus wants to reveal Himself and the Father to you. Jesus wants you to come to Him with the things that hinder your ability to humble your heart to His word. You humble your heart to Jesus through a life of obedience to His Word. Jesus wants you to use the power of His grace against the things that hinder you so you will be free. Because you are free, you will learn to avoid wickedness, evil thinking, and scheming. Then Jesus will reveal His Father to your soul.

LESSON: *Just as Jesus reveals His Father to humanity, God wants you to reveal Jesus to humanity. You are in partnership with the Lord, and He has made you an ambassador for that purpose.*

When Apostle Paul learned of the sincere faith of the Ephesians believers and the love amongst them, he prayed that God would give them the spirit of wisdom to know Him by revelation. As I indicated in Chapter 1, Jesus is the wisdom and the power of God that you need. Therefore, you need these abilities from Jesus to know God the Father and to overcome life distractions that hinder your life of obedience.

Ask God for more of Jesus, His wisdom, in your inner being, which is equivalent to more of the Holy Spirit, the Spirit of Grace.

LESSON: *A revealed knowledge of the Father and Son will have a lasting and life-changing influence on your daily life pursuits. It will orient your entire life to diligence in your Christian living, which will always uphold obedience and the fear of the Lord as priorities.*

In Christ alone will you find your life's meaning and divine definition as the true redeemed—as a new creation. The Bible says you live, and move and have your being through Jesus (Acts 17:28).

Chapter 5
The Grace of God and Salvation

The Bible says the grace of God brings salvation. By God's unmerited favor, you have received salvation. According to Romans 5:10, "For if when we were enemies we were reconciled to God by the death of His Son, much more, now that we a reconciled, shall we be saved by His life." For by grace you have been saved through faith, and that not of yourselves, it is the gift of God, not of works, lest anyone should boast.

While you, and all humanity, were an enemy to God, you were reconciled to God by the death of Jesus Christ the Son of God. You are reconciled to God through Jesus' sacrifice on the cross. God will save you from wrath to come on all the rebellious and wicked. After being reconciled to God, you choose to live in and through Jesus.

LESSON: *Because God is going to save you from His wrath against the rebellious, ensure you refuse a rebellious life after salvation.*

You Are Reconciled To God

The Bible says in 2 Corinthians 5:19, "That is, that God was in Christ reconciling the world to Himself, not imputing their trespasses to them, and has committed to us the word of reconciliation." See yourself as reconciled to God. He has made you an agent of reconciliation for Jesus Christ.

Again, through Jesus Christ and through the blood of His cross, there is now peace between you and God. It pleased the Father to reconcile all things to Himself through Jesus, whether the things on the earth or the things in heaven. Therefore, see yourself as reconciled to God through Jesus Christ. Your responsibility is to continue in the faith, stable and steadfast, not shifting from the hope of the gospel.

Grace and Righteousness—Your Victory in Life

The Bible says in Romans 5:17, "For if by one man's offense death reigned through the one, much more those who receive abundance of grace and the gift of righteousness will reign in life through the One, Jesus Christ". In Christ Jesus and by God's unmerited favor, He has ascribed to your new creation, the gift of righteousness and grace.

In the first Adam, heaven sees you as dead. You were without the life of God. However, in Christ you have the promise of life. With grace and righteousness, you are set up to reign in this world over anything it will throw at you. No weapon fashioned against you shall succeed (Isaiah 54:17). Therefore, practice and grow in your righteous lifestyle.

In fact, through Jesus Christ, by whom you have received grace, all the promises of God find their fulfillment. By God's divine favor, He has established you in Christ and He anoints you and puts His seal on your life by the Holy Spirit as a guarantee of His ownership.

The grace of God is available to every human on this planet Earth. The Bible says in Titus 2:11, "The grace of God that brings salvation has appeared to all men". Because the grace of God brings salvation, it implies every human is a candidate for salvation. God is not willing that any should perish, but that all should come to repentance (2 Peter 3:9). No wonder Jesus commands His followers to reach out to the whole world with the Good News of God's favor of salvation.

Repentance opens people up for the abiding Word of the Gospel, which grows their knowledge of God. Repentance also makes the salvation of a person genuine.

LESSON: *To claim to have salvation without repentance will produce a fake and weak Christian lifestyle.*

Grace and the Call to Total Surrender

It is by the grace of God, the unmerited favor, that you receive salvation. The part you play in this process is your genuine repentance. To repent is to forgo your previous evil and disobedient ways of living.

In salvation, God gives you a measure of faith as a gift through His spirit. It places a burden on your heart to accept what you hear from the proclaimed Gospel. When you accept God's gift, the spirit of belief enters your heart to yield you to the Good News.

LESSON: *To believe is not just a mental process or mental orientation. To believe in the Gospel of your salvation is total surrender of your heart to the Savior Jesus Christ. It is an unspoken covenant you make to live the rest of your life for Jesus and through Him alone.*

You do not have to live your Christian life for a long time before realizing you aught to live for Jesus, and through Him. It is the grace of God, which helps you come to this realization. Until then, you could easily yield to ungodliness and worldly lusts.

LESSON: *God deals with you at the level of your knowledge of who you have become in Jesus Christ. Therefore, the Bible commands you to add knowledge to your faith. Faith without knowledge is weak faith. You will be up one day and down the next.*

As you increase in knowledge of your identity in Christ, and you yield to its demand on your life, Jesus gives you wisdom to understand a deeper knowledge of the Kingdom to which you now belong. Your obedience to the Gospel grows your understanding of the power available to you through the grace of God. Because your heart continually yields to the Gospel of Jesus Christ and the epistles of the disciples, the Holy Spirit leads you into a deeper knowledge and understanding of the call to Kingdom matters, especially the call to the kingdom of heaven.

You will come to know, that your life as a Christian is not just to attend church, but the Kingdom of heaven has a demand on your total life and lifestyle, even your thought processes. Growth in knowledge helps you know your identity in Christ and the need to desire more of the grace of God. You will regard God's grace as an indispensable force you need each day.

LESSON: *If you are fully committed to Jesus Christ in your heart, the power of the Spirit of God will manifest and be evident in your life. You will have access to the rich resources that the gospel presents to you.*

Learn to surrender your entire heart to Jesus Christ after salvation. You may yield your heart to preaching and teaching that elevates your hopes for the greater things of God. However, you need encouragement to surrender your all to Jesus. Hope without total surrender could be empty hope.

Chapter 6
Learning to Commune with the Spirit of Grace

The God and Father of the Lord Jesus sent the Holy Spirit, the Spirit of Grace, to help you in your life issues. The Bible says this about the Spirit of Grace, "Anyone who has rejected Moses' law dies without mercy on the testimony of two or three witnesses. Of how much worse punishment, do you suppose, will he be thought worthy who has trampled the Son of God underfoot, and counted the blood of the covenant by which he was sanctified a common thing, and insulted the Spirit of Grace?" (Hebrews 10:28-29)

Jesus said this about the Holy Spirit, "Therefore I say to you, every sin and blasphemy will be forgiven to men, but the blasphemy against the Spirit will not be forgiven to men. Anyone who speaks a word against the Son of Man, it will be forgiven him; but whoever speaks against the Holy Spirit, it will not be forgiven him; either in this age or in the age to come".

LESSON: *It is more important to be a friend of your helper, your comforter, the Holy Spirit, than an enemy. This way, you will learn not to blaspheme against the Holy Spirit.*

Benefits of Hearing from the Spirit of Grace

Again, Jesus said in John 14:26, "But the Helper, the Holy Spirit, whom the Father will send in My name, He will teach you all things and bring to your remembrance all that I have said to you." Know the following about the Holy Spirit, the Spirit of Grace:

- He is holy and the Spirit of Truth, who leads you in the path of holiness if you will learn.

- He teaches you all truths.
- He reminds you of all that Jesus taught in His Gospel.
- He witnesses about Jesus through you to others.
- He reminds you all that Jesus wants you to know.
- He baptizes you with power. Jesus said, "But you shall receive power, when the Holy Spirit has come upon you; and you shall be witnesses to Me in, and in all and, and to the end of the earth" (Acts 1:8).

LESSON: *As you grow in the knowledge of the message of Jesus, you will come into a state of peace. This peace is not as you will find in the world.*

The current age of self and competitiveness places a demand on you to grow in your ability to identify accurately the voice of the Holy Spirit. This will help you live within the boundaries Christ has assigned to you. It also helps you avoid deception.

Learn the way of Jesus

The Bible says this about Jesus, "And His delight shall be in the fear of the Lord. He shall not judge by what His eyes see, or decide disputes by what His ears hear."

Many things go on in the world today, because some people's desire is to exert self, which oftentimes results in conflict with other people. When a person has conflict with another, they usually will say defaming words about that one. Normally, these are untrue words.

LESSON: *As you grow towards Jesus' way of His interpersonal relationship, you will grow and cease judging life situations by what you hear from people and by what you see with your eyes.*

Your ability to judge by what the Holy Spirit says to you will always be the truth and far from falsehood and personal vendetta. In my own life, I would not disclose what other people tell me to my own wife because I do not know how she would handle what she hears me say, either internally or outwardly. The only time you can say to another, what you hear from people or what you see with your eye is when the Spirit of Truth, the Holy Spirit, confirms it. Even then, He has to give you the go ahead to do so. Remember that God is in the process of transforming us into the image of Jesus Christ, His son.

Speaking to the crowd, someone in said to Him, "Teacher, tell my brother to divide the inheritance with me." But Jesus said to him, "Man, who made me a judge or an arbitrator over you?" Jesus, knowing all the ways of men, went on to talk about covetousness. He said, "Take heed, and beware of covetousness, for a man's life does not consist in the abundance of the things which he possesses".

Therefore, grow in your ability to hear from your only one helper, the Holy Spirit sent to you from God through Jesus Christ.

The Spirit of Grace and your Life

The greatest university you can attend in this Kingdom business is the "University of the Holy Spirit." It is not a formal way of education, which issues a diploma upon your completion. However, He is able to make you grow in insights and understanding of the kingdom heaven. If you orient your ears to hear Him (as Jesus did), and your mind and heart to understand Him, you will learn that the Holy Spirit is the best teacher of this age.

Normally, your formal Bible school education helps you know how to tune your ears, your mind, and your heart to receive from the Holy Spirit. Jesus said the Holy Spirit, the Spirit of Grace, will teach you all truths, and bring to your remembrance all that Jesus, spoke and taught. What is greater than to gain insight into all that Jesus taught? I recommend Bible education of some kind to all who want to learn to hear the Holy Spirit.

As I indicated above, what you learn from Bible colleges helps tune your ears, mind, and heart to the greatest teacher, the Holy Spirit, the Spirit of Grace. If you learn to yield to His training, the Spirit of Grace will turn you, though common you are, into a spiritual giant in this world.

LESSON: *If you learn to yield your life to Jesus, the Holy Spirit, the Spirit of Grace, is able help you walk in the power of His presence—the resurrection power.*

Grow your faith, so your faith would become genuine. Read 2 Peter 1:5-7. With your genuine faith, Jesus will make you strong, and you will manifest the power of Christ in your life, and in your ministry. He will train you, and make you into a conqueror and a Kingdom-minded child of God who has the power to enforce justice, obtain promises, stopped the mouths of "lions," quench the power of fire, escape the edge of swords, become strong out of your weakness, become mighty in war, and put foreign armies to flight. You will not fear torture and you will refuse unfaithfulness to secure your release. You do all these things so you might rise again to a better life.

God Helps You by His Spirit

When God promises to instruct and teach you the ways in which you should go, He does this through His Holy Spirit, the Spirit of Grace. God says to you in Psalm 32:8-9, "I will instruct you and teach you in the way you should go; I will counsel you with my eye upon you. Do not be like a horse or like a mule, which has no understanding, which must be harnessed with bit and bridle, else they will not come near you."

God wants you to understand Him because you are His child. A child is required to understand the father. Therefore, God deals with you as His child, not like a mule or a horse. God instructs and teaches you by His Spirit.

The Bible says, "For it is God who works in you both to will and to do for His good pleasure. Do all things without complaining and disputing, that you may become blameless and harmless, children of God without fault in the midst of a crooked and perverse generation, among whom you shine as lights in the world" (Philippians 2:13-15).

LESSON: *Do not train yourself as the child of God who grumbles and complains about everything you do not understand about God's work in your life.*

The circumstances in your life may sometimes feel tough, and you may not know what to do. However, the best thing to do is to draw closer to Jesus through prayer, with the help of the Spirit of Grace. He has grace for you to overcome.

If you complain and question, you question God's management of your life. Therefore, seek grace to help you understand the God who has saved you and is making you into image of Jesus Christ. You are His child and He loves to be close to you. Learn from Jesus, when it was hard on Him, He said to the Father, "Your will be done".

God desires to help you in your life issues. In your battles in life, your challenges, and in your daily Christian life, God wants to be part of all you do. He wants to get involved with everything you do. He counsels you to present your body a living sacrifice, holy, pleasing to Him, which is your reasonable service. He wants you to not be conformed to this world, but be transformed by the renewing of your mind, so you may prove what is that good and pleasing and perfect will of God (Romans 12:1-2).

LESSON: *Conformity to the ways of the world is a huge problem for many of God's people. The reason is that many do not orient their minds and ears to hear the spirit of God.*

LESSON: *You are not pursuing a religion, but a relationship with the Living Christ. He wants to be involved with all you do. He does this through His Holy Spirit, the Spirit of Grace.*

The voice of the Holy Spirit comes clearly to your renewed mind. His voice brings to you understanding of the will of God for your life and ministry. The God who has called you is Spirit and your mind has to renew, and become kingdom minded. This is how you will understand the will of God, who is Spirit.

To renew your mind, you need the grace of God to do so. The Word of God is spirit and life, which will teach you and give you wisdom, and train your conscience to differentiate between corruptible things, so you pursue only those things that will edify you. The power of the grace of God will enable you to stand strong in your current life situations, so you would live faithful to your Redeemer.

Chapter 7
The Grace that Jesus Gives

As a Christian, Christ has given you gifts and called you to function in diversities of ministries. You may have one or more gifts. The military will give a soldier the best of their equipment to function effectively. Likewise, Christ provides you a measure of His grace, per the gift and calling He has assigned to you. This grace helps you accomplish all He has assigned to you; including the office, He calls you within His church. Christ gives His gifts to His people to equip them to accomplish effectively, all of His calling.

The calling of God is first your journey to His eternal glory and gift He has assigned to you for His body. Jesus provides you grace in proportion to the gift He has given you: "But to each one of us grace was given according to the measure of Christ's gift" (Ephesians 4:7).

Writing to the Romans, Apostle Paul said we have different gifts according to the grace that Christ has given to us. If it is prophecy, do so in proportion of your faith; or in giving, with liberality; or if you lead, do so with diligence; or if you are the one who shows mercy, do so with cheerfulness.

Grace to Avoid Competition

It is very important to note that Jesus provides grace according to the gift, and the calling He has for your life. This knowledge will remove competitiveness and rivalry from your heart. To compete with another is to envy God's glory in his or her life. Never allow such a mindset to enter your heart because you may not know the disciplines the brother/sister has endured at the hands of the Lord to walk in His

anointing or calling. You may also lack the knowledge regarding v
the Lord began His work in his or her life.

The Pharisees saw Jesus grow before their eyes and when God b﹍g﹍
to work mightily through Him, they envied Him. They would come
down on anyone who sang the praises of Jesus. In John 12:10-11, the
chief priests plotted to put Lazarus to death, for because of him, many
of the Jews went away and believed in Jesus.

LESSON: *Do not compete with or envy Christ's gifts or His work in
another's life. You have to set your heart right and ask the Lord for what
you want. He will not deny you any good thing that will make you effective
in your Christian life or in the function of your gifts.*

If you compete with others for what Christ is doing through them,
the Bible calls you unwise. In 2 Corinthians 10:12, the Bible says this:
"For we dare not class ourselves or compare ourselves with those who
commend themselves. But they, measuring themselves by themselves,
and comparing themselves among themselves, are not wise." Learn to
defy the devil when he entices you to compete with another Christian
for what Christ is doing through them. The Bible says competing with
others is earthly, sensual, and demonic. It is a self-seeking spirit and not
wisdom from God.

Grace to Fulfill God's Purposes and Assignments

When Jesus redeemed you by His blood, God "rewired" your
new creation for His divine purpose. For that reason, Jesus provides
you grace to help you do God's will, to His pleasure. Therefore, learn
not to measure yourself with others and the grace they have received
from Jesus.

Apostle Paul disclosed what God has "rewired" him to do. He said
in 1 Corinthians 3:10-13, "According to the Grace of God which is
given to me, as a wise master builder, I have laid the foundation, and
another builds on it. But let each one take heed how he builds on it. For
no other foundation can anyone lay than that which is laid, which is
Jesus Christ. Now if anyone builds on this foundation with gold, silver,

precious stones, wood, hay, straw, each one's work will become clear; for the Day will declare it, because it will be revealed by fire; and the fire will test each one's work, of what sort it is."

Christ gave Apostle Paul the grace of God to help him build the foundation for today's Church. He cautioned that you must take heed to what you build on this foundation, even your life, because Christ will subject it to His testing fire, to reveal the sort of work you have built.

Apostle Paul confessed the grace of God made him who he was and the grace he received was not in vain. By saying the grace he received was not in vain, Apostle Paul meant he utilized the grace of God to its maximum. He pleaded with the Lord to remove his limitations so he could stretch out to do more, but the Lord said to him, "My grace is sufficient for you, for my power is made perfect in weakness" (2 Corinthians 12:9).

LESSON: *Do not use the words of the Lord to Apostle Paul to stay in your weakness. Apostle Paul was pressing deeper into Christ with the grace he received. This must be your attitude, to press deeper into Christ through knowledge, truth, righteousness, and sincere love for Jesus and for people.*

Apostle Paul said, "I worked harder than any of the other apostles." Even then, he admits that it was not he, but the grace of God given to him. Therefore, Apostle Paul acknowledged that none of His hard work was from his natural abilities, his learning, or his degrees, but the grace of God.

The grace given to him helped him endure life's reproaches, persecutions, and distresses, for Christ's sake. This made him strong.

LESSON: *What do you do in your life as a Christian? Are you running a church or a ministry with much success, or do you have victories left and right in your life? Do you sometimes yield to the temptation of measuring yourself against others? The good things that happen for you in your life come to you through the power of God's grace.*

Just like Apostle Paul, Christ gives grace to help you fulfill His assignment for His church.

Ephesians 3:7-8 states, "Of this gospel I was made a minister according to the gift of God's grace, which was given me by the working of His power. To me, though I am the very least of all the saints, this grace was given, to preach to the Gentiles the unsearchable riches of Christ."

Other people can see the grace of God on your life. In his second letter to the Galatians, Apostle Paul wrote, "And when James and Cephas and John, who seemed to be pillars, perceived the grace that was given to me, they gave the right hand of fellowship to Barnabas and me, that we should go to the Gentiles and they to the circumcised".

Grace of God and Faith for Life and Ministry

Everything you do in your Christian life and ministry is by the grace of God. Apostle Paul said in 1 Corinthians 15:10 that the grace of God made him who he became, and that helped him to labor more abundantly than everyone else, yet he confessed it was not by his natural abilities, but the grace of God which was with him.

LESSON: *Never see what God has assigned you to do as more important than everyone else. If you fail to see yourself as nothing without the grace of God, the spirit of competitiveness can enter your heart to cause trouble.*

LESSON: *Whatever you are going to become in Christ is by the grace He provides and the grace you seek.*

Apostle Paul said in 2 Corinthians 12:11, "I have become a fool in boasting; you compelled me. For I ought to have been commended by you; for in nothing was I behind the most eminent apostles, though I am nothing."

Apostle Paul understood the grace given to each to accomplish Christ's assignments and purposes. Apostle Paul understood that, though there is one Lord, one faith, and one baptism, Christ has given to each grace, which is in proportion to the measure of the gift He has given. That is why the Bible says when Jesus ascended on high; He gave gifts to men.

When you have received the gift from Christ and His grace, it becomes your responsibility to seek to advance in what He has assigned to you. You seek more grace to do so because God wants His fullness to indwell you. The fullness of God in you will perfect His assignment through your life. Therefore, do not say to yourself at any time that you know it all. This is when pride could sneak into your heart, to make you think your life or ministry is more important than others' are.

In your quest to do God's will, you may come against many challenges and difficulties. In all these, learn to stand firm and to set your eyes on the God who called you. He will take care of your situation. He is the helper for your life situations.

LESSON: *You cannot say you understand what God has assigned you to do until you begin to take baby steps towards what He says to you.*

You must know and understand that no matter where you are in the doing of God's assignment, He is the one who supplies all you need in the spiritual, physical, and even financial issues. Apostle Peter prayed for multiple of grace and peace to you, because life comes with diversities of difficulties and challenges as you pursue God's will.

Paul realized that there are diversities of gifts, which Jesus gives. These gifts and callings differ according to the grace Christ has given you. The grace given to you will activate a level of faith you need for the function of your gift and the calling, which Christ has for your Christian life. Even then, the Bible encourages you grow your faith by adding some attributes.

The Bible says to you if your gift is to prophecy, if it is providing service, if it is teaching, exhortation, contributing to the needs of others, leading a group or a church, and so on, you have to grow your faith for an effective functioning of your gift. God has opened the throne of grace to you. Go there boldly to seek mercy and find grace to function in your gift and calling with the highest integrity and humility.

The level of proficiency in the function of your gift or calling is by the grace of God. You do what you do well as a Christian because the grace of God provides you the ability to do so. This is why you can do all things through Jesus Christ, who strengthens you. Therefore, it leaves no room for boasting or competitiveness. When you fail to acknowledge the grace of God as the source of your strength, it is likely that pride can enter your heart causing you to think you are who you are by your own effort or learning.

The Lord will caution you when that happens. However, if the focus of your heart is to glorify self, and to make money with your gift or calling, you may ignore the caution the Lord gives.

Whenever you ignore the cautions of the Lord for misusing your calling and gifts, you could end up dispensing His gifts for your financial gain. Consequently, there will be an exchange spiritually. God will not take His gift from you, but the evil one could corrupt your gift, and deceive you to think God is still working through you, when it is false. God does not work with exalted hearts.

This is why the Bible commands you to let your love for God be genuine. If Christ has called you to function in His Kingdom, your love for Him must be strong through a life of obedience. Romans 12:9-10 says this: "Let love be without hypocrisy. Abhor what is evil; cling to what is good. Be kindly affectionate to one another with brotherly love, in honor giving preference to one another." The Lord requires you to function in His calling, and with His gift given to you, with love and humility.

LESSON: *Do not entertain the idea that the number of years you have been a Christian is what qualifies you to function in any of Christ's gifts. It does not work that way! Christ who gives you spiritual gifts and the grace needed to empower you with what you can do effectively.*

The Bible says in Ephesians 4:8-12, "When He ascended up on high, He led captivity captive and gave gifts to men. ... And He Himself gave some to be apostles, some prophets, some evangelists, and some pastors and teachers, for the equipping of the saints for the work of the ministry, for the edifying of the body of Christ".

If you do all that the Lord enables you to do with your heart drowned in the "sea of love", for Christ and for people, the Spirit of Grace will assist your ministry. He will help you manifest love at a higher level, in the humility of heart, and with Christ's power. Consequently, you will not regard what you do as greater than the calling of others.

Apostle Paul wrote to the Corinthians, "The eye cannot say to the hand, "I have no need of you"; or again the head to the feet, "I have no need of you. And those members of the body which we think to be less honorable, on these we bestow greater honor; and our un-presentable parts have greater modesty". Let the janitor fail to keep the house clean and litter will be all over.

The Bible counsels you in Romans 12:3, "For I say, through the grace given to me, to everyone who is among you, not to think of himself more highly than he ought to think, but to think soberly, as God has dealt to each one a measure of faith."

If you perform your function with love, God's grace will help you overlook the faults and offences of people, even your enemies. That way, you will serve them with the gift of the Lord without becoming selective.

LESSON: *The Lord requires you to workout His calling, and gifts with love. In love for God, and for people, you will acknowledge the source of your abilities in His Church. You will not see other calling or gifts as less than your own.*

Know that your enemies are not other Christians. Your enemies are the wicked, who hate the Jesus in your life, many of whom are unbelievers! If you view your fellow Christian as your enemy, you are walking in a diminished understanding of your identity in Christ, and His call to you to love one another. Your enemies must be unbelievers and not other Christians. Even then, Christ commands you to love your enemies.

Are you able to sing, and people fall under the anointing of God through you? Always remember that it is the Spirit of grace working through you. Are you the one who write books that changes the lives of many people? Remember, it is the Spirit of grace who works through you!

The Grace of God and Humility

The knowledge or revelation Apostle Paul received, that it was the grace of God that made him who he was had an influence on his life and his view of ministry. It kept him humble in heart. Learn Apostle Paul's way of thinking. The Bible calls on you to have the mind of Christ

Jesus, the humility and ability to evaluate yourself correctly within God's divine order (Philippians 2:5-9). Your consistent life of humility in your Christian life comes with God's promotion. You need to seek grace to live a humble life in all of life's situations.

LESSON: *It is very important to acknowledge that whatever abilities you have that helps you in your function in this Christian life, is not you but the Grace of God.*

Jesus said you could do nothing apart from Him. It is not by your intellectual abilities or by your educational degrees. It is only by the grace of God and the power of the Holy Spirit. If the functions assigned to you are to open blind eyes, raise the dead, or heal the lame and crippled, you must learn to live with a humble heart. If you need more grace, talk to Jesus and tell Him about your heart's desires.

LESSON: *To pride yourself for what you do or the functions Christ has assigned to you is an indication that you think your hands or the number of years you have been a Christian is what gives you the abilities you have. That thinking is false! It is only the grace of God working through you. Therefore, be humble!*

Whenever you pride yourself for what Christ through the power of the Holy Spirit is doing through you, the power of the anointing could depart from you. You could come into the state the Bible calls "Ichabod", which means God's glory has departed. If you have a large church, it is by God's grace. If you have a very dynamic and effective ministry, it is by the grace Jesus Christ has given you.

If you understand all mysteries and you know the ways of God, it is by the grace Jesus has provided you. If you clearly understand these facts or truths, it will leave no room for boasting about your ministry or church. You will deny Satan from taking advantage of you to corrupt God's grace and anointing in your life or ministry. Jesus provides this grace for the sake of others because He wants to make Himself known to them through you.

The Bible says in Luke 17:7-10, "And which of you, having a servant plowing or tending sheep, will say to him when he has come from the field, 'Come at once and sit down to eat'? But will he not

54

rather say to him, 'Prepare something for my supper, and gird yourself and serve me till I may eaten, and drink'? "Does he thank that servant because he did the things that were commanded him? I think not. "So likewise you, when you shall have done all the things which you are commanded, say, 'We are unprofitable servants. We have done what was our duty to do.'"

LESSON: *It is for the sake of others that Christ has given you His gifts and His ministry. It is not to place you on the pinnacle of your self-ego.*

Jesus said in John 14:10, "Do you not believe that I am in the Father and the Father is in me? The words that I say to you I do not speak on my own authority, but the Father who dwells in me does His works." Likewise, Jesus works through you by the power of His Holy Spirit, the Spirit of Grace.

The seventy disciples returned from their mission trip rejoicing that the demons were subject to them in Jesus' name. Jesus drew their attention to the fact that what they did was His authority given to them. The thing that must motivate you to rejoice is not what Jesus does through you, but the fact that you have your name engraved in the books of heaven.

In Matthew 18:3, Jesus wants your attitudes and your responses to life to become like a child. This is what Jesus says about humility. In the Kingdom journey, you do not prove to anyone your worth, no matter who you are in life or in church. You do not prove you are the boss of your life. It is by the grace of God that has made you who you are. Therefore, God wants you to pursue life with humility of heart. God requires you to do what is just, pursue mercy towards others, and to walk humbly before Him (Micah 6:8).

If you are not a person redeemed by the blood of Jesus, your attitudes in life could be different. However, because you are redeemed and received the power of God's grace, He expects humility and a righteous approach in your attitudes and responses in life to be different from those in darkness. Jesus says to you that humility is one of the doorways to the kingdom of heaven and into your greatness (Matthew 18:4).

If you have difficulty humbling yourself or your heart in life, go to Jesus because He has grace to help you. Then you will be able to take His yoke upon you. The yoke of Jesus is His gentleness and lowliness of heart. Jesus said His yoke would provide rest for your soul. This is how you can remain calm and restful in your life issues. It keeps you from a frequent state of anxiety.

Jesus cautions those who have received His grace but fail to yield to the power of grace, to continue in their own ways but He is coming quickly with His reward for what everyone has done.

LESSON: *The Lord's "quickly" may not be as the world defines quickly. The Lord's quickly may last for years, seasons, or ages. All that time, He gives you the opportunity to repent of any inconsistencies in your life, and to do His will.*

The Grace of God and Truth

It is important to know that the grace of God came with truth: "And we beheld His glory, the glory as of the only begotten of the Father, full of grace and truth". Therefore, to seek the grace of God is to walk in truth also. You cannot claim to walk in grace or have grace, and yet, walk in falsehood. If you are in grace, your lifestyle, and your ways must show the light of Christ, a life of truth.

Talking about himself as the truth of God, Jesus said in John 7:18, "He who speaks from himself seeks his own glory, but He who seeks the glory of the One who sent Him is true, and no unrighteousness is in Him". Unrighteousness is falsehood. In unrighteousness, people operate in the "dark", away from the light, lest their falsehood becomes exposed.

LESSON: *To operate in the dark does not mean literal darkness. Do not train yourself to operate in the dark with rudeness because you think many of God's people focus on the flesh and do not see or care about what the Holy Spirit says to them.*

Jesus said in John 3:20, "For everyone who does evil hates the light, and does not come to the light, lest his deeds should be exposed". Therefore, all you do in this life, must bear witness that you are in the light of Christ, that is, you live in Jesus, who is true. This is so because you have received the grace of God to live in truth. People who operate with falsehood serve a master, Satan, whether they know it or not.

How to Seek the Grace of God

You seek God's grace through prayer. As I indicated a few times earlier, you seek the Word of God that relates to your situation. Then, through prayer, you seek His wisdom, and the power you need to triumph over or for your breakthrough in your situation. That way, you will not corrupt or defile yourself. You seek the Word of God because the Word will give you the knowledge, and the understanding of the will of God that relates to your situation. Once you have received the Word of God, you must trust Him for wisdom, and His power to overcome your situation.

The Bible calls on you to come boldly to the throne of grace to seek mercy and find grace to help you confront your time of need. When you come to the throne of grace, you seek for mercy because oftentimes your ways stray away from the standards God has set for your redeemed life in Christ.

Seeking for mercy is like pleading for forgiveness in areas where you fall short. With your restoration to righteousness, and with the grace you receive from the Lord, you are rightly set up to reign over your situation. Come to the throne of grace boldly, but not in arrogance. Humble your heart in the presence of Jesus. Then you ask for His wisdom, and His power to help you confront and overcome your current problems or challenges.

You do not have to confront your situation by yourself. If you do so, you may sometimes overcome your situation. However, in the process, you could corrupt yourself in other areas of your life. That is not what God wants for your redeemed life. You need the wisdom and the power of God to confront your current life situation in righteousness, and godliness after the Word has given you direction to your solution. That way, you will not corrupt yourself. Corruption takes you out of holiness.

Job said in Job 28:20, "From where, then, does wisdom come? And where is the place of understanding?" Then he concluded in Job 28:28, "Behold, the fear of the Lord that is wisdom! And to depart from evil is understanding!" As I indicated earlier, Jesus is the "door" to the throne of grace.

LESSON: *Do not be deceived; if you live your life lacking the fear of the Lord, you lack wisdom and understanding. For those who walk in the fear the Lord, He gives them wisdom to know some things about life in this world.*

You have to learn to treasure up the Word of God in your heart, and seek it like you would the world's silver. Then, the Word will lead you into many Kingdom values in the Lord.

A New Law and the Grace of God

Jesus said in Matthew 5:17, "Do not think that I have come to destroy the law or the prophets. I did not come to destroy but to fulfill." The law gave the children of Israel how to live and conduct their lives, after their deliverance from bondage in ancient Egypt.

Today, if you are born again by the Word and spirit of God, you have a greater law, the law of the Spirit of life, which you must learn to obey. This law is in Jesus Christ, and functions through the voice of the Holy Spirit. He instructs and teaches you in the ways of righteousness, of holiness, of godliness, and truth. The practice of these attributes helps you avoid another law that entangles the fallen nature. It is the law of sin and death, which disables the ability of people outside of Christ so they would not obey God.

However, you are a born-again child of God—redeemed by the blood of Jesus—and you overcome the law of sin and death through Jesus Christ. The Bible says in Romans 8:1-2, "There is therefore now no condemnation to those who are in Christ Jesus, who walk not according to the flesh but according to the Spirit. For the law of the Spirit of life in Christ Jesus has made me free from the law of sin and death." Because the law of the Spirit of life is at work in you, and you live by the Holy Spirit's directions, and not by the flesh, you escape condemnation.

This law of the Spirit of life in Christ Jesus produces fruit, which transcends every law. The Bible says in Galatians 5:22-23, "But the fruit of the Spirit is: love, joy, peace, long-suffering, kindness, goodness, faith, meekness, self-control. Against such there is no law." These are the fruit you bear if are submitted to the law of the Spirit of life in Christ Jesus.

LESSON: *The fruit produced by the law of the Spirit of life in Jesus Christ is so powerful, if it works in your life, no law can take you down or discourage you to live unfaithful to your Redeemer.*

Jesus said the Holy Spirit is your helper in these matters. He said in John 14:26, "But the Helper, the Holy Spirit, whom the Father will send in my name, He will teach you all things and bring to your remembrance all that I have said to you". The Holy Spirit is the Spirit of grace, and He teaches you all things, and brings to your remembrance all you know but may have forgotten. This work of the Holy Spirit happens in your life issues so you can avoid lawlessness. Lawlessness displeases your Savior, Jesus Christ, and His Father.

It is important that you learn to identify the voice of the Holy Spirit. His voice speaks to your spirit in your prayer time. His voice comes also to you in your problems and challenging times, as well as the good times. He is the voice of Philippians 2:13, who work in you to help you work and do what pleases God.

It is therefore necessary that you learn to identify the voice of the Holy Spirit's within your spirit. You have to fashion yourself with the grace of God to help you hear His voice. When you hear, you have to obey because He is the Spirit of God who works in you to will and to do what pleases God.

LESSON: *To say you did not know when you did wrong is an indication you need to grow more in identifying the voice of the Holy Spirit, because He spoke to your heart before you engaged in your wrongdoing.*

LESSON: *The new law works with the life of righteousness. The Bible calls you blessed and satisfied if the hunger in your Christian life is for righteousness.*

The Ministry of Jesus—an Example

In addition to all that Jesus did, including the miracles He performed, He never lacked the practice of righteousness and holiness.

The Bible says in Romans 1:3-4, "Concerning His Son Jesus Christ our Lord, who was born of the seed of David according to the flesh, and declared to be the Son of God with power according to the spirit of holiness, by the resurrection from the dead".

In Hebrews 1:8-9, the Bible says this about Jesus, "Your throne, O God, is forever and ever; the scepter of righteousness is the scepter of your kingdom. You have loved righteousness and hated wickedness; therefore God, your God, has anointed you with the oil of gladness beyond your companions." Jesus practiced righteousness and holiness in His life issues. He hated wickedness and lawlessness!

LESSON: *Wickedness is to know the actions or deeds that honor God, even what the Holy Spirit communicates to you, but you choose to do what pleases self. It is lawlessness!*

Jesus said to the Jews in John 6:38-40, "For I came down from Heaven, not to do My own will but the will of Him who sent Me. This is the will of the Father who sent Me, that of all He has given Me I should lose nothing, but should raise it up again at the last day. And this is the will of Him who sent Me, that everyone who sees the Son and believes in Him may have everlasting life; and I will raise him up at the last day".

Amazing Statement by Jesus

Jesus said in Matthew 7:21, "Not everyone who says to me, 'Lord, Lord,' shall enter the kingdom of heaven, but he who does the will of My Father in Heaven".

Then in Matthew 7:22-23, Jesus said something that could amaze you, if you walk as He walked, and function in His power as He did. He said, "Many will say to me in that day, Lord, Lord, have we not prophesied in Your name, cast out demons in Your name done many wonders in Your name? And then I will declare to them, 'I never knew you; depart from me, you who practice lawlessness!'"

We know some of the things Jesus did in His ministry when He was with us in bodily form. In Luke 7:21-22, He sent to tell John the

Baptist the miracles his messengers saw Him do. The messengers from John the Baptist witnessed Jesus heal the blind, restore those with infirmities and afflictions, cleanse lepers, heal the lame, raise the dead, cast out evil spirits, and preach the gospel to the poor. We also know that He prophesied many times, with examples found in Matthew 12:40, Matthew 17:27, and Luke 19:30-32.

Jesus said prophesying and doing great miracles alone in His name does not open heaven's gate to you. In Luke 10, Jesus sent out seventy of His followers on a mission trip. They came back rejoicing that the demons were subject to them in Jesus' name. Jesus said to them in Luke 10:19-20, "Behold, I give to you authority to tread on serpents and scorpions, and over all the power of the enemy, and nothing shall by any means hurt you. Nevertheless, do not rejoice in this, that the spirits are subject to you, but rather rejoice that your names are written in heaven."

Jesus pointed out that it is good to prophesy and to do miracles, but in addition to doing so, you must ensure your name is in the books of heaven. I will therefore help you understand why it is possible to do mighty works of miracles, and yet have your name missing from the books of heaven.

You may say, I do not prophesy and I do no miracles so I am all right! However, before you develop this sense of security, you must understand that prophesying, casting out demons, and healing the sick are all gifts Jesus gives to His Church, which includes you. Therefore, do not consider those who function in these gifts or callings as a bad thing. Apostle Paul encourages you to pursue love, and earnestly desire the spiritual gifts, especially that you may prophesy.

Moreover, your new creation has made you an ambassador for Christ Jesus. As an ambassador, learn to yield your life to your home country. Your home country is in heaven. Therefore, learn to please your home country, to please Jesus who has given you the ability or the authority to do miracles, and function in His gifts.

It is therefore important to find answers why Jesus made the statement in Matthew 7:22-23. To do so, you have to understand some things. You have to know you have become a new creation whose attributes are godliness, righteousness, and holiness. These attributes constitute power or authority in the spiritual realm. No wonder God commands you to practice them in your life issues. Moreover, you are an ambassador for Christ, and ambassadors do not live carelessly! Therefore, you need grace of God to orient your life and lifestyle to please Jesus.

Correct Placement of Focus

It is very important that you do not completely set your entire focus only on what Jesus is doing through you. Whether it is the exercise of your gift or what you do in His church, His body. Always remember that it is the grace of God, which helps you do all you do in His church or your ministry. If you fail to know who works in and through you, you could ignore the grace of God you need to seek to help orient your life, lifestyle, attitudes, and behaviors to God's pleasure. The Bible says neither circumcision nor uncircumcision matters. Rather, what matters is being a new creation.

The correct focus is to find grace to live in ways His work in you remains powerful, and that His grace is changing your inner character to God's pleasure. Christ will do His work through you, so your central focus must be on growing in the attributes of your new creation. In all that you do with the grace of God given to you, you "must be *made*." The goal of God for you is your sanctification, and transformation into the image of His Son, the submitted and obedient One.

Therefore, God reminds you in Galatians 6:7-8, "Do not be deceived God is not mocked; for whatever a man sows, that he also will reap. For he who sows to his flesh will reap corruption, but he who sows to the Spirit will of the Spirit will reap everlasting life."

LESSON: *You do not go to heaven because of the grace of God Jesus gives to you for ministry. Rather, you go to heaven because you find grace to avoid lawlessness in your life after you have used the grace of God Jesus gives to you. God looks for inner and outward sanctification.*

God expects you to seek grace to help you live your Christian life in obedience to Him. He says in Hebrews 12:28 to seek grace to serve Him acceptably. You serve God acceptably through a life of obedience, and in godly fear. No matter the level of grace Christ has given you for what you do in life or in the church, God wants your life to meet His expectations as the redeemed of the Lord.

No matter the degree of Christ's grace to you and the level of your function—the number of blind eyes you open, the number of sick people you heal in Jesus' name, or the accuracy of your prophecies—in the end, Jesus could say to you, "I do not know you."

LESSON: *The life of righteousness and godliness will not permit you to live as though this world is your heaven. In addition, it will not permit you to live with a worldly lifestyle.*

Your life of righteousness also overcomes covetousness and competitiveness—the ungodly cravings for what others have. You corrupt your soul if you ignore God's command! Christ will reward you for the fruit you produce with what He has ascribed to you, recorded in Ephesians 4:24.

Failure to live your life constrained within the boundaries of righteousness, holiness, and godliness, is the reason Jesus would say to you, in the last day, "I never knew you; depart from me, you who practice lawlessness!" Christ rewards you for the fruit you produce out of what He has inputted into your new nature. You produce fruit from these attributes because you practice them in life.

LESSON: *Lawlessness is an indication you are living a life that pleases your self, and not Jesus. Jesus rewards you according to the fruit you bear out of the attributes He has imputed to your new nature or new creation.*

In addition, you must understand the difference between the works of ministry, and the works of righteousness. It will help you use the grace you seek from Jesus to orient your lifestyle and all that you do to satisfy Jesus.

The Works of Ministry

As I indicated earlier, Christ gives you grace for all your abilities and all you do as a Christian, which is by the grace Christ gives you.

Apart from Jesus, you can do nothing to God's pleasure. It is not by your educational degrees or efforts.

The works of ministry is therefore, what the grace of God helps you do in your Christian life and ministry. These involve miracles and mighty deeds, preaching the Gospel to others, and prophesying. Jesus wants you to function as He did.

In addition, the works of ministry is to live as a faithful steward of what Jesus Christ has given or assigned you to do. Note that to have wonderful works of ministry is not necessarily fulfilling the works of righteousness.

Works of Righteousness

The works of righteousness is the grace you have to seek to help you handle life issues with righteousness. This way, your behaviors, attitudes, and thought-processes will conform to the attributes of your new creation, the new self in this world. It helps you handle your personal and interpersonal relationships in truth, in righteousness, in holiness and in godliness. With the grace you seek from the Lord, your deeds will reflect the characteristics of your new life, which are righteousness, holiness, and godliness. You will learn to do all these in humility, truth, and in the fear of the Lord. This is one of the reasons God commands you to put on the attributes of your new creation in Christ.

In addition, in the works of righteousness, you must seek the grace of God to help you keep your attitude towards the things of the world under check, especially money. You find grace to help you keep your interpersonal behavior in the confinement of righteousness, godliness, and holiness, all to God's pleasure.

Your works of righteousness enhances your maturity in holiness. It also enhances your walk in the fear of the Lord. The pursuit of righteousness overcomes the attitudes and behaviors that corrupt your life all over again. Your victory over corruption in this world enhances your walk in the fear of the Lord. In the fear of the Lord, you cease to live an unrighteous life.

In works of righteousness, you strive for peace with all men and pursue holiness. You grow in your ability to control the tongue. You must also understand that those who pursue peace sow Jesus' fruit of righteousness. You must learn humility to walk in peace with all people.

In the works of righteousness, you find grace to workout your own salvation. How do you work out your salvation? You find grace to put off your old attitudes, behaviors, and mindsets because God has recreated you anew. You are not the same person you were before Christ. You are a new creation! The Bible says in 2 Corinthians 5:17, "Therefore, if any one is in Christ, he is a new creature; old things have passed away; behold, all things have become new."

At the same time, you find grace to renew the spirit of your mind, to help you avoid practicing the attributes of your old nature. God wants you to practice in your life issues, who He has made you in Christ Jesus, all in a life of truth.

To put off the old attitudes, lifestyles, manners and thought processes are not as easy as it shows on the pages of the Bible. It constitutes the Christian warfare. To put of your old self and to renew the spirit of your mind, and to put on the new self demand that you seek grace to do all these. By the power of God's grace in Christ, you fight daily to obey His command.

What is Lawlessness?

Lawlessness is the failure to submit or the refusal to submit to the dictates of God's Word and the voice of the Holy Spirit in your life issues. Remember King David. He said in Psalm 119:11, "Your word I have hidden in my heart that I might not sin against you". The Word of God in your heart will guide you in the ways of obedience, and hence, the way of righteousness.

Never train yourself to become one of those in the world, or in the church, who avoid God's Word so they can fulfill their own selfish inner drives. Learn to permit God's Word to place constraints or boundaries on your inner drives. Failure to do so, will place a 'chill' on your love for God; hence, your love for people. Your submission to God's Word measures your love for Him (1John 5:3).

LESSON: *Love for God is not just to know His Word, but the Word must constrain your life in obedience to Him.*

Obedience is a life-long process of learning, not only in your Christian life today, but also for eternity. Once you learn the art of obedience to God, it never ends. Obedience is required in heaven as well! You must therefore learn to live your Christian life with less complaining and questioning.

You corrupt your life if you are the child of God who complains about and questions everything. If you have chosen to learn obedience, it helps you learn to do God's will consistently like your Master Jesus. Growing in your ability to obey God consistently is an indication that you are conforming to the image of Jesus, the Son of God.

Obedience is a dynamic force, which is able to activate the presence of God and Jesus in your life. If your obedience ceases to grow, it freezes and begins to self-destruct, corrupting your life all over again.

Grace to Overcome the Spirit of Saul

God has showered His goodness on you and has provided His grace through Christ Jesus to help you overcome in this dark world of disobedience and self-will. He wants you to define your daily Christian living in obedience to His Word and promises. Failure to obey Christ as a lifestyle will bring you into a serious realm.

There are many evil spirits in this dark realm of the world. They help people who refuse to obey Christ to pursue a selfish and disobedient lifestyle. You have to seek the grace of God from Jesus to help you overcome envy and hate, which the passage in 1 Samuel 18 indicates about King Saul towards David. The engines that drive evil in this world are hate and envy. You are in the world, but do not belong to it.

Hate and envy could open doors into your life, giving opportunity for evil spirits to create rooms in your heart again. Once they do so, they are able to access these rooms every time you hit crossroads, and your self-interest is at stake.

David prayed to God to create a clean heart in him. A clean heart is able to practice the yoke of Jesus. A corrupt heart exalts itself against God's Word in life's crossroads and when your selfish interests are at stake. I believe you understand what I am trying to communicate to you in the above passage. Therefore, I believe you will seek grace to help you avoid hate and envy in your life.

LESSON: *Whenever an evil spirit creates a "room" in your heart, there will be reoccurrence of hate and envy anytime you see someone do something you desire to do but have not yet received the grace to do. Other times, hate and envy takes over your heart whenever your selfish interest is at stake. Note that selfish interests are never the Lord's interest. Also, watch out for recurrent behaviors and attitudes!*

Grace to Overcome Ungodly Ambitions

The prophet Samuel anointed David to become the next king after King Saul. Unfortunately, King Saul was seeking to destroy David. As recorded in 1 Samuel 24, David had the opportunity to eliminate the threat of King Saul, which could have opened the door for David to become king immediately. The prophet Samuel was around to authenticate him as the next king.

Even though David had the opportunity to eliminate King Saul, he restrained himself and allowed God's timing to run its course. David said to King Saul in 1 Samuel 24:9-13, "Why do you listen to the words of men who say, 'Behold, David seeks your harm?' Look, this day your eyes have seen that the Lord delivered you into my hand in the cave, and someone urged me to kill you. But I spared you, and I said, 'I will not stretch out my hand against my lord, for he is the Lord's anointed.'"

"Moreover, my father, see! Yes, see the corner of your robe in my hand. For in that I cut off the corner of your robe, and did not kill you, know and see that there is neither evil nor rebellion in my hands, and I have not sinned against you. Yet you hunt my life to take it. Let the Lord judge between you and me, and let the Lord avenge me against you. But my hand shall not be against you. As the proverb of the ancients says, 'Wickedness proceeds from the wicked.' But my hand shall not be against you."

LESSON: *Learn not to pursue your ambitions with an ungodly heart. Like David, let the timing of God play out for what He has ordained for your life.*

LESSON: *According to the ancient saying, do not allow wickedness proceed out of your heart to ignore God's timing in your life pursuits. You have the grace of God to help you wait for God's timing in all issues of your life.*

In Jude 1:16-18, the Bible says, "These are grumblers, complainers, walking according to their own lusts; and they mouth great swelling words, flattering people to gain advantage. But you, beloved, remember the words which were spoken before by the apostles of our Lord Jesus Christ: how they told you that there would be mockers in the last time who would walk according to their own ungodly lusts".

God has you on His schedule and He will not deny you any good thing. He says to you in Psalm 84:11, "For the Lord God is a sun and shield; the Lord gives grace and glory. No good thing will He withhold from those who walk uprightly." Therefore, seek the grace of God to help you avoid ungodly ambitions.

Learn from David! Do not allow fleshly ambition to compel you to seek what you think God has ordained for you. I know there are times you will know exactly what God want you to do for your breakthrough. If you are not sure, do what God is telling you in Philippians 4:6-7. God says in this passage not to be anxious about anything. He says in everything to make your ambitions known to Him through prayer, supplication, and thanksgiving. He will hide your mind and heart at peace in Christ Jesus.

Understand that anxiety can make you hurry yourself ahead of the timing of God and you could get yourself into pursuits and things that corrupt your life. The grace of God is available to you through Christ Jesus. The Lord is your only source of supply in this life and He will provide all you need. You do not have to allow ungodly ambitions to drive your heart to hurry yourself ahead of God's timing. The Bible says to you in Psalm 27:14, "Wait for the Lord; be of good courage, and He shall strengthen your heart; Wait, I say, on the Lord!"

Claiming Grace or Under Grace

As I indicated earlier, if you claim to be in grace or under grace, you are declaring to the whole world, including beings in the spiritual realm, that you have received the power, the Word, and the wisdom of God to triumph in this age. These attributes represent Jesus Christ, the grace of God, to the whole humanity. This is why the Bible says the grace of God that brings salvation has appeared to all men.

Your claim of being in grace and under grace also implies you have received God's ability through Jesus Christ to overcome ungodliness and worldly lust. In addition, your claim also implies you have received God's ability through Jesus Christ to live soberly, righteously, and godly in the present age.

Likewise, your claim announces that you have received the grace of God from Jesus to do whatever He has assigned to you and your ministry with the highest integrity, righteously and godly. This, in effect, is the reason the grace of God is the final solution, to help us triumph over inconsistencies in our pursuit of God's will.

When Jesus came on the world scene, the grace of God not only became God's unmerited favor to save and to redeem, but also the Word, the power, and the wisdom of God that humanity needs to serve God acceptably and to do His will. Moreover, the grace of God teaches the redeemed to live a triumphant life in this world of corruption, and to overcome self-driven tendencies.

Through Jesus Christ, God has established a new order. What we thought was impossible has now become possible through the power of God's grace. You are now able to worship God in spirit and in truth because you have received the Holy Spirit, who is the Spirit of Truth and the Spirit of Grace. You are able to serve God in the ways He desires because of His grace available to you through Jesus Christ.

God accomplishes all things through Jesus Christ by the power of His Spirit. The Spirit of God is so vital in God's mode of operation, that Jesus said those who blaspheme against Him never receive forgiveness.

Therefore, seek grace to help you orient your spiritual ears to hear the voice of correction from the Holy Spirit, the Spirit of Grace. Be willing to do the corrections He commands you. Also, always find grace to help you to practice the attributes of your new nature.

Remember what Apostle Paul did with the grace he sought in Christ Jesus, which he said in 1 Corinthians 9:27, "But I discipline my body and bring it into subjection, lest, when I have preached to others, I myself should become disqualified."

Disqualification implies, Jesus could say to you in the last day, "...I never knew you, depart from me, you who practice lawlessness". Disqualification is not only for ministry workers but for you as well. Seek grace to orient your life to do God's will to avoid Jesus' statement that He never knew you.

Chapter 9
Called to the Throne of Grace

If you are saved by the grace of God, then you will need more daily graces to help you live a victorious Christian life in this corrupt and evil world. The grace of God will help you live in the light of your new creation. You cannot live the true Christian life without the grace of God. Therefore, God says to you in Hebrews 4:16, " …Come boldly to the throne of grace, that we may obtain mercy and find grace to help in time of need."

Diversities of Life's Challenges and Grace of God

Your salvation does not give you the permission to live any way. Neither is grace the reason you live any way! The Bible says in 1 Corinthians 10:23, "All things are lawful for me, but not all things are helpful; all things are lawful for me, but not all things edify." Therefore, you will need the grace of God to help you identify things that will edify, and those that will not.

You will need a daily "dose" of the grace of God to help sustain you in the diversities of life issues that you confront. That way, you will avoid living like the Adam generation, which is your old ways. God has made provision of grace for your daily challenges. Therefore, God expects you to live like a champion through the power of His grace in Christ Jesus. You will be able to live a victorious Christian life in this corrupt and evil world. The grace of God will help you live in the light of your new creation, and is one of the reasons why, in many of Apostle Paul and Peter's letters to the churches, they would begin by extending grace and peace to them as a way of salutation.

God has opened the gate to the throne of grace to help you come boldly to seek for more grace in your time of need. In every life challenge or difficulty, God has a special grace for you to overcome. The Bible says in Romans 5:20-21, "Moreover the law entered, that the offence might abound. But where sin abounded, grace abounded much more, so that as sin reigned in death, even so might grace reign through righteousness to eternal life through Jesus Christ our Lord."

Therefore, God has every grace you may need to overcome Satan's enticements to defy your loving Jesus through disobedience and lawlessness. In the process, you will learn to do God's will, no matter the intensity of the contentions you face in this life. Oftentimes, God permits these contentions to test your resolve to stay obedient to the Redeemer, Jesus Christ.

LESSON: *The many ungodly and unrighteous deeds and behaviors among God's people are because many lack the presence of God the Father and His Son. They draw their strength from their intellectual abilities. They have not truly yielded to Jesus Christ. They even lack knowledge of the call to the throne of grace.*

It is important as the redeemed of the Lord, to understand why the contentions. This way, with the grace of God, you would stay resolute and faithful to your savior. In your desire for grace, God will grant to you a measure of His Word, His wisdom, and power for all you do, so you can do His will through the power of the Holy Spirit. This way, you will please God in all you do.

Understand that life in this world has diversities of evil and challenges. Therefore, you need to seek grace to confront all of your life issues and challenges so you will do the will of God. If you seek grace to help you, you will not fall.

LESSON: *To fall does not mean you cease going to church. You could be in church and yet have hidden issues that eat you up spiritually or mentally.*

Therefore, God commands you to come boldly to the throne of grace to obtain mercy and to find grace to help you in your life issues. If you are born-again or not, you need more of God's grace if you desire to live to please God. The Holy Spirit will help you overcome the many challenges, and evil inclinations in the world, even the motivations that comes from self.

LESSON: *To seek the grace of God is to seek the wisdom, the power of God, and a Word from the Holy Spirit to help you in your particular life situations.*

This must become your lifestyle as the redeemed child of God. Fortunately, you have the Holy Spirit as your indispensable helper, who is here to assist you do the will of God. He exalts Christ in and through your life, and must therefore become your best friend in your journey through this life.

He takes what is of Christ, and helps you do what Christ requires of you, in the power, in righteousness, and godliness to God's pleasure. This is how you overcome every life issue, which could pose a challenge to your sound life in Christ. Many of these life issues seek to diminish the significance of your identity in Jesus Christ. First, it steals the Word of God in your life in order to confuse you of your identity in Christ Jesus. When the Word in your life remains diminished, your strength also diminishes.

Always be courageous and bold to walk in the authority you have from Christ Jesus. Pray daily for more of God's grace and peace, inwardly and outwardly!

After redemption, God calls on you to serve Him acceptably. Apostle Paul received this revelation, that the God you desire to go to in heaven is a consuming fire of absolute holiness and righteousness. What does God expect from you who want to come to Him? God requires all who desire His kingdom in heaven, to serve Him acceptably. What is the acceptable way to serve God? He says you do so through a life of obedience (reverence) and godly fear. In fact, the grace of God is what you need to do everything God wants from your redeemed life.

Seek More of the Grace of God

God, according to His abundant love for humankind, has raised the throne of Jesus Christ, as the platform by which He shows His mercy, and provides grace to all people who call on Him. You come to the throne of grace first to seek God's mercy for any inconsistencies in your life, and then find grace to help you in your times of need.

Your time of need could be the challenges you face in life while doing the will of God. It could be physical, mental, emotional, or financial. Oftentimes, you forget to yield to God's command because of lack of knowledge on how to come to the throne of grace. Coming to the throne of grace could involve a few ways, such as the following:

- Prayer and fasting: if you are disposed to do so, and the Bible encourages you in Philippians 4:6, "Do not be anxious about anything, but in everything by prayer and supplication, with thanksgiving, let your requests be made known to God". To supplicate could involve pleading with God. Pleading with God could involve fasting!
- Bother God by your constant praying. God wants to be bothered! God's desire is that you will effectively use the opportunities He gives you in Jesus' name. He wants you to use every grace you can get at the throne of grace to help you overcome in your life challenges. That way, you will not fail to please God in your life's challenges.

LESSON: *The many inconsistent lifestyles you pursue as a Christian is due to the unwillingness, the failure, or the ignorance regarding the throne of grace God has willingly opened for you, the redeemed of the Lord.*

Because you are born-again, you need more of God's grace, if you desire to live to please God. He, the Holy Spirit, the Spirit of Grace, will help you overcome the many life challenges and evil inclinations in the world, even the motivations that comes from self.

To seek more of the grace of God is to seek more of His Word, His wisdom, and His power, which Jesus represents. Therefore, to seek more of God's grace is to seek more of Jesus in your life. To seek more of Jesus in your life translates to more of His Holy Spirit, the Spirit of Grace. Also, grow your life of obedience, to the Word of God.

The Holy Spirit is here to exalt Christ. He takes delight in all who exalts Christ in their lives. Because you have yielded your life to Jesus, the Holy Spirit helps you do what Jesus wants, in power and wisdom, without deviating from the Word, all to the pleasure of God.

This is how you would overcome in every life issue in this world. Many of these life issues seek to diminish your strength as the redeemed of the Lord, who has an identity in Jesus Christ. Your identity in Christ Jesus is a very powerful being, which you have to know and walk in it.

To say you need multiples of the grace of God, and peace in today's world can never be overemphasized. Pray daily for more of God's grace and peace! To do so, you have to learn to pray more in your daily life. You do not necessarily go and kneel down to pray. Because God is spirit, He hears you even when you are in a situation where you cannot kneel and pray.

Comparing Manna and the Grace of God

The most important journey you will ever undertake is the journey from your day of redemption to the kingdom of heaven. In this journey, you can encounter various trials and difficulties. Apostle Peter said God is testing the genuineness of your faith. This is the reasons for the many trials you go through in your Christian life. The reward is always glorious. Your faith makes you shine like polished gold, though your experiences may seem like going through Christ's fire. However, the result produces praise, honor, and glory at the revelation of Jesus Christ.

Moreover, the Bible says that you could go through many problems and difficulties to enter the kingdom of heaven. Therefore, seek the grace of God to help you build yourself strong in your faith.

Then the Lord said to Moses, "Behold, I am about to rain bread from heaven for you, and the people shall go out and gather a day's portion every day, that I may test them, whether they will walk in my law or not" (Exodus 16:4).

God fed the children of Israel with manna in their journey from the Red Sea to their Promised Land. Similarly, God has you in a journey from your day of redemption and you are on your way to the kingdom of heaven. This journey comes with various trials and temptations, which God has the power of grace (manna) to help you endure.

Jesus said in John 6:32-33, "Most assuredly, I say to you, Moses did not give you the bread from heaven, but my Father gives you the true bread from heaven. For the bread of God is He who comes down from heaven and gives life to the world". Jesus is the true bread from God the Father. He came into the world to give life to a world that has become spiritually dead. Jesus came into the world full of the power of God's grace. Everyone who finds or believes on Jesus receives the life of God.

The life in Jesus is as manna from heaven, to help sustain your life in this turbulent world, so you would do the will of God. You cannot do the will of God by your own strength. You do the will of God only by the grace of God in Jesus Christ. He said in John 6:27, "Do not labor for the food which perishes, but for the food which endures to everlasting life, which the Son of Man will give to you, because God the Father has set His seal on Him".

In Exodus 16:4, God said, He will test the children of Israel, if they will keep His law or not, that is, if they will keep instructions concerning the fetching of manna—"Behold, I will rain bread from heaven for you. And the people shall go out and gather a certain quota every day that I may test them, whether they will walk in my law or not." Today, with the open door policy of God, concerning the throne of grace, God test you to see if you would do the following, among others:

1. If you desire to do His will for your life, because those who desire to do the will of God are those who will frequent the throne of grace.
2. If you are serious about the heavenly calling, which begins with the call to workout your salvation, and to grow in genuine faith.
3. If you appreciate your deliverance you received by the shedding of Jesus' blood, which took you from darkness into the light of Christ.

God test you to see if you will heed His call to come to the throne of grace, to seek a "quota" of grace for each day. You need the grace of God daily because each day comes with its own trials and difficulties.

Jesus said in Matthew 6:34, "Therefore, do not worry about tomorrow, for tomorrow will worry about its own things. Sufficient for the day is its own trouble." Therefore, you need grace for each day's challenges. Seek for fresh grace each day.

LESSON: *When you grumble about the difficulties and troubles you face in your Christian life or the work of God in your life, you disregard the fact that He knows what is best for your life.*

LESSON: *If you appreciate your salvation, and desire to go to heaven, you will frequent the throne of grace to help you find the Word, the wisdom, and the power of God to help you overcome in your life challenges.*

The experiences of the wilderness proved that the children of Israel carried the slave mentality. There is abundance of knowledge compiled in the Bible. Therefore, do not continue to lack knowledge of God's good intentions for your life, in this journey to heaven.

LESSON: *If you continue to wallow in the attitudes of your past, you have not overcome the mentality of your past—you still have the slave mentality of your past.*

God calls on you to seek His grace, just as He instructed Moses about manna in the wilderness. You will need the grace of God until you leave this life. In the kingdom of heaven, you may not need grace in the dimensions as defined on earth. In heaven, your completeness becomes a reality, and you will have no devil to entice you to disobey God.

The Bible says in Exodus 16:35, "The children of Israel ate manna forty years, until they came to an inhabited land; they ate manna until they came to the border of the land of Canaan".

Moses said to the children of Israel in Exodus 16:19, "Let no one leave any of it till the morning". Notwithstanding they did not heed Moses, and some of them left part of it until morning, and it bred worms and stank, and Moses was angry with them. This is an indication you need fresh grace of God each new day.

LESSON: *The grace of God, which you need for your today's challenges, may not sustain you for the issues of your tomorrow.*

Remember the Throne of Grace

God commanded, and Moses instructed Aaron to "Take a pot and put an omer of manna in it, lay it up before the Lord, to be kept for your generations". Therefore, Aaron laid it up before the Testimony, to keep it there. The omer of manna that was kept, served as remembrance throughout their generations, so that they may see the bread with which God fed the children of Israel for forty years in the wilderness, when He brought them out of the land of Egypt." Therefore, the manna sustained the children of Israel for forty years until they entered the Land of Promise.

The grace of God will sustain you in this life of many challenges, until you leave the earth. Therefore, never forget the throne of grace. God invites you to come to find grace for your daily life issues. You need a measure of grace daily, for your life issues, if you desire to please God in your ways.

For you, upon whom the end of times has come, the daily fetching of manna serves as an example and a reminder that you daily have an open door to the throne of grace. So long as you live in this world, and in this body, you will not cease to need the grace of God daily. It is your only way of triumph in the world of ungodliness and fleshly pleasures of evil.

Grace, the Power of God You Need

The power of the grace of God is what you need to triumph in this world, and to accomplish heaven's demand on your life as the redeemed. Irrespective of the lawlessness in this world, the power of the grace of God will help you overcome through righteousness. The grace of God gives you the ability to serve God the way He desires through Jesus Christ. Jesus is your only source of grace and your only ability to serve God, and satisfy the demands of the glory coming to you when Jesus returns. Apart from Jesus, you can do nothing to God's pleasure.

There are overwhelming challenges in this world, which seek to diminish your significance in Jesus, and to tear you down from your enviable place in Jesus—God's divine order for you in Jesus. The grace of God therefore becomes your indispensable source of strength, to live and to please God in ways He desires. The grace of God is the source of your triumphant Christian life, because in Him, there is a greater law that overcomes any other law that could drag your life into fleshliness after your redemption.

You cannot ignore the power God has for you in His grace, Jesus Christ, if you desire to possess your inheritance reserved for you in heaven. It is by the power of grace that you are able to fulfill every demand on your salvation without unfaithfulness to God.

God knows your life will encounter many needs, first as a human in this flesh and blood body, and secondly as the redeemed called to live a life pleasing to your Redeemer and His God.

Therefore, you will need to find grace for every life issue. This will help you handle your life issues to God's pleasure. In this Christian life, no one can overcome or conquer apart from the grace of God. As I indicated earlier, the grace of God is the power of God's Word, His wisdom and the power of the Holy Spirit, the Spirit of Grace.

Jesus sent the Holy Spirit from His Father to empower the redeemed to live soberly, righteously, and godly in this age of the world, where corruption and evil motivations run rampant. God provides this grace through Jesus Christ as His final solution, for the possible inconsistent lifestyle you could fall into as you tread along the path to life—to heaven.

Chapter 10
The Grace of God and the One You Serve

Through Joshua, God reminded the children of Israel all He had done for them from the time of Abraham to their current state (Joshua 24:1-13).

LESSON: *It is very important to remember the things God has done in your life in the past, so you do not become discouraged in your current life experiences.*

If you make this acknowledgement of God's work in your life a part of your lifestyle, you will learn to continually fear Him and hence, live faithful to Him. God desires faithfulness and sincerity from all who claim to serve Him. He commands you to examine yourself to see if you are in the faith. God wants you to test your faithfulness and sincerity to Him.

God's command gives you the opportunity to know if you are growing in your ability to define your daily choices and decisions by His Word and precious promises.

LESSON: *If you lack faithfulness and sincerity to God, it is an indication you are holding back some areas of your life, which you have not yielded to Him.*

Joshua's Challenge to God's People

In Joshua 24:14-15, Joshua threw a challenge to the children of Israel, saying, "Now therefore fear the Lord, and serve Him in sincerity and in faithfulness. Put away the gods that your fathers served beyond the River and in, and serve the Lord. And if it is evil in your eyes to serve the Lord, choose this day whom you will serve, whether the gods your fathers served in the region beyond the River, or the gods of the Amorites in whose land you dwell. But as for me and my house, we will serve the Lord."

LESSON: *When God permits you to do anything, it does not necessarily imply He accepts what you do. That is why He asks you to refuse the world conforming you into her mold. Rather, He wants you transformed by renewing your mind, so you will discover His will for your life.*

It is so important to remember the transaction that took place for your redemption. Jesus shed His blood, amid suffering, to purchase your redemption. In your life, learn to have answers to the following three questions:

- Am I walking in the fear of the Lord?
- Am I serving the Lord in sincerity of heart?
- Am I serving the Lord in true faithfulness?

Unlike Joshua's day, you have abundance of God's grace to help you live a sincere, faithful life, all in the fear of the Lord. If you have chosen to serve the Lord who redeemed you by His blood, then acknowledge that you are not of your own any longer. You now belong to the One who purchased you by His blood. He purchased you from the power of darkness to belong to His God.

When Joshua challenged his people to choose the god they will serve. They responded in Joshua 24:16-17, "Far be it from us that we should forsake the LORD to serve other gods; for the LORD our God is He who brought us and our fathers up from the land of Egypt, from the house of bondage, who did those great signs in our sight, and preserved us in all the way that we went, and among all the people through whom we passed". What a great confession and testimony from the children of Israel in response to Joshua's challenge. It is a common saying that we must mean what we say and say what we mean!

God, through the sacrifice of Jesus Christ, has redeemed you from the power of darkness, where Satan held you captive to evil, sin, and self. He has transferred you to the kingdom of His Son, the kingdom of Light. God's expectation for you is that you will live through Jesus, in His light, and serve God in the fear of the Lord. Therefore, you must serve God in the sincerity of your heart. It must not become an outward show, which has no substance.

When your service to God lacks sincerity or genuineness, you could switch to unfaithfulness in your very difficult and challenging seasons. It must be the opposite—you must learn to press deeper into Jesus, like a tree in a dry place. When the environment feels harsh, and it senses water in the ground, it sends its root deep into the ground to contact the water.

Jesus says you must have root in yourself, so you can endure the harsh seasons, when Satan seeks the Word in you. He brings tribulation or difficulties, and persecution into your life to see if you will buckle and fall away, giving up the Word you have received (Matthew 13:20-21). Note that the goal of the devil is the Word in you, which he knows can make you strong to overcome him.

Confronting Whom You Serve

Usually, men have different levels of ego. Therefore, after salvation, it is important to verify which of the three kingdoms (listed below) your lifestyle offers allegiance to.

1. The kingdom of God
2. The kingdom of the world
3. The kingdom of SELF

A kingdom has a king and the king has rules that his subjects must obey or live by. If you serve God, you know that He has rules recorded in the Bible that you must study daily, so you would learn to live by. The Bible says God, has given you His very great and precious promises to live by. It will help you escape the corruption that comes into your life by lustful desires (2 Peter 1:4). When you escape corruption, your spiritual life grows, and you begin to manifest the divine nature of God, which is your new creation.

By God's promises, you can increase your focus on the things of God and hence, serve Him acceptably. The cravings for the things of the world bring you under subjection to the king of the world, Satan. The fuel that propels the cravings for the things of the world, are the powers of darkness. This is the reason the Bible commands you to not love this world. Love for the world is enmity against God.

Apostle James wrote, "Adulterers and adulteresses! Do you not know that the friendship of the world is enmity with God? Therefore whoever desires to be a friend of the world is the enemy of God" (James 4:4).

If your mind is set on the things of the world, your actions, and deeds will fail to please God, which can lead to fleshly mindedness. The fleshly mind is not subject to God's Word (Romans 8:7).

The Deception of Serving Self

Oftentimes, you think you know God because you know His Word. However, the truth is simple! You do not know God unless His Word is having influence on your personal life, and interpersonal relationships, and your life issues, to God's pleasure. In addition, the Word you know must affect how you handle the things of this world.

In some instances, you know the Word of God; however, your responses to life's demands, and to people, along with your attitudes and behavior remain questionable, because they deviate from God's expectations. This is not an indication that you know God. The Bible says in 1 John 4:20, "If anyone says, I love God, and hates his brother, he is a liar. For if he does not love his brother whom he has seen, how can he love God whom he has not seen?" To hate your brother is to love him less!

King Saul's Example of Living for Self

A biblical example of disobedience to God and living for self is King Saul. He was Mr. Nobody when God's grace found him. The Prophet Samuel anointed him to become king over God's people, .

Saul prophesied with the prophets the day that Samuel anointed him. This is a sign of God's grace on his life. Unfortunately, he allowed self, disobedience, envy, and hatred to destroy the greatness God had for him and his family.

LESSON: *As a redeemed child of God, never allow disobedience, envy, and hatred to have any foothold in your life, because you know, and understand the unmerited favor of God that saved you, and cleansed your many sins.*

King Saul consistently disobeyed God's direct command to him. God therefore chose David as a future king to replace Saul. King Saul's life of envy and hatred for David began when the women came out to welcome Saul and his army after the defeat of Goliath, and the Philistines. These women came out of the cities singing, "Saul has slain his thousands and David his ten thousands" (1 Samuel 18:7). This song displeased Saul very much, and it made him very angry and jealous towards David.

In 1 Samuel 18:8, Saul regarded what these women said as evil. He said to himself, "They have given David ten thousands, and to me they have given only thousands. And what more can he have but the kingdom?" Because of Saul's attitude towards David, an evil spirit came upon him, who tormented him daily.

LESSON: *The Word of God is His direct command to you. You must therefore learn to keep and act on those you know, and the ones the Holy Spirit brings to you in your life issues.*

LESSON: *What is your demeanor when people praise another and you think you should have received the honor? Do you allow evil to enter your heart?*

LESSON: *Anger and jealousy are a direct disobedience to God's expectation for you in your interpersonal relationships. Never allow these attitudes to entrap your Christian life.*

God has told you in the book of Micah, what is good! He requires that you do justice, and to love kindness, and to walk humbly before Him. Envy and jealousy could come into your life, whenever you see someone else do what you desire to do, but do not yet have the grace to do so. Sometimes, it comes into your heart when your selfish interests are threatened.

Note that selfish interests are not the Lord's interest. The Bible commands you in Proverbs 4:23, "Keep your heart with all diligence, for out of it springs the issues of life". Things in your heart will eventually reflect in your behaviors, and attitudes in your interpersonal issues.

The Bible says Saul eyed David from that day on. To eye someone is to be jealous of that person. The next day a harmful spirit from God rushed upon Saul, and he raved within his house while David was playing the lyre, as he did day by day.

LESSON: *A harmful spirit came from God into the life of Saul, because the Bible says in Proverbs 16:4 (RSV), "The Lord has made everything for its purpose, even the wicked for the day of trouble."*

The orientation of Saul's heart placed him among the wicked, which opened him up for the wicked spirit to come upon him. The Bible says to watch over your heart because the issues of life flow from it.

Saul had his spear in his hand, and he hurled the spear, for he thought, "I will pin David to the wall". However, David evaded him twice. Saul was afraid of David because the LORD was with him, but had departed from Saul.

Today, you have grace through Jesus Christ to overcome jealousy, and hatred, which constitutes a life of disobedience to God's word. If you are born-again and living for Jesus, you do not have to fear anything in life, even when life threatens your hopes in the world. Every good gift, and every perfect gift is from above (James 1:17). Jesus said to you not to fear because He has overcome the world. John the Baptist said in John 3:27, "A man can receive nothing unless it has been given to him from heaven".

LESSON: *Your obedience to the word of God, though you do not see Him, deepens your life and position in Jesus. You mature in the life of righteousness and hence, holiness. (Romans 6:16-19).*

LESSON: *In the pursuit of your selfish agenda, you may ignore the interest of your nation if the Lord shows you the prevailing situations in your nation.*

The Deception of Serving the World

To serve the world is to seek or crave for more of the things of the world, to the neglect of the things of God. Oftentimes, the heart craves for more of the world's goods, and pleasure more than the cravings for the things that matters most, things that would prepare you for the kingdom of heaven.

Apostle Paul wrote to Timothy that the time would come when people will become despisers of good, lovers of worldly pleasure, rather than lovers of God. However, because you are born-again, these lifestyles must not become a part of you.

The Bible says Christ in you, is the hope of glory. Jesus Christ is the only dynamic power, and force in the whole of the universe, by which you can grow in your desire for God without hindrance. Apart from Jesus, you have no power against the pull of the world; in fact, apart from Him, you can do nothing to God's pleasure. Your delight in the things of God makes you a vessel He can use to help others (Isaiah 58:12).

God has ordained that at the mention of the name of Jesus, every knee in heaven, and on earth and under the earth should bow and every tongue confess that Jesus Christ is Lord to the glory of God the Father. Therefore, nothing in this world can help you or sustain your life for your journey to eternity, but Jesus only.

Understand that Jesus does not come in your life to stay dormant. He expects you to acknowledge His presence, so you will allow Him to lead you in a life of love, humility, righteousness, in your interpersonal and personal life issues. These lifestyles are opposite to the ways of the world. The world thrives on malice, deception, and outwitting one another with hidden jealousy.

Serving the World is Serving Satan

When your life yields to the craziness of this world, you may, in ignorance be submitted to the king of the world, Satan. Do not let your delight for the things of the world lead you to obey his demands. There is much excitement and pleasure in Jesus. If you understand your new identity in Jesus, you will find in Him enough to delight your soul.

LESSON: *Do not allow the world to define what your God can do for you. Let the world know that your God can do exceedingly abundantly above all you can ask or think, according to His power that works in you.*

If you are Kingdom minded, going to church is always a delight to your soul. You know you will hear something that will draw you closer to your destiny. Therefore, serve the Lord with a delightful heart and do not draw your delight from the ways of the world.

Serving God through the Power of His Grace

To serve God requires obedience. The Bible says in Hebrews 12:28, "Therefore, since we are receiving a kingdom that cannot be shaken, let us have grace, by which we may serve God acceptably with reverence and godly fear."

The lifestyle that pleases God is a lifestyle of obedience to His Word, no matter what the world presses on you to do otherwise. Your desire to obey God's Word will orient your heart to walk in the fear of Him. Therefore, a life of obedience and godly fear is what God demands of all who serve Him.

There are many benefits for those who live with the fear of the Lord in their hearts. The Bible says in Psalm 34:7-10, "The angel of the LORD encamps all around those who fear Him, and delivers them. Oh, taste and see that the LORD is good; blessed is the man who trust in him! Oh, fear the Lord, you His saints! There is no want for those who fear Him. The young lions lack and suffer hunger; but those who seek the Lord shall not lack any good thing."

In the spiritual realm, obedience to God's Word invites His presence, because it represents the fear of Him. The Bible says to reverence God, which is to obey Him in all life issues, even in challenging and difficult times. This is a heart issue because obedience is a heart issue! You deceive yourself if you have no reverence of God deep down in your heart, but only dwell on an outward show of commitment to Him.

LESSON: *Anything that has a prominent place in your heart will orient your heart to commitment to that thing. Such a thing could become the god you serve. Therefore, orient your heart to learn obedience to the word of God, and enjoy His presence enthroned on your heart.*

In the spiritual realm, things do not take that much time to do as is in our physical realm. Satan showed Jesus all the kingdoms of the world in a moment of time. He offered to give to Jesus all the authority and glory of what he just showed Him. It is very interesting, the very rewards God set before Jesus is what Satan offered to Jesus to receive His worship.

LESSON: *Take heed to the things the devil convinces you to do for your glory and authority, even for your ego. They could be the very things God has already promised to give you for your life of obedience.*

The Call to Serve God with Reverence

God wants you serve Him with reverence and godly fear. To serve God acceptably with reverence is a call to a life of obedience to His written Word. You will obey the one you reverence. If you reverence God, you will obey Him. However, you do not see God! Notwithstanding, God has written His Word to you. The Word of God is God.

If you receive a memo from your company's CEO, you will not request to see the CEO before you do what the memo says to you. You will do what the memo commands. Similarly, if you reverence God, you will obey the "Memo" He has written to you (His Word you know from the Bible).

Obedience to God's Word is unknown, but it shows up in your life situations, events, and issues. When you face challenges in life, your obedience to God's Word will become clear. As you learn to obey God in your life issues with the grace you seek from Him, Jesus enlarges in your life. The more of Jesus in you, represents more of the Holy Spirit in your life. With more of the Holy Spirit in your life, you will receive an inner strength to obey God.

The Call to Serve God with Godly Fear

Another way of serving God acceptably is to seek grace to serve Him with godly fear. Godly fear is not being scared of God. Godly fear was the delight of our Lord Jesus Christ. The Bible says in Isaiah 11:3, "And His delight shall be in the fear of the Lord. He shall not judge by what His eyes see, or decide disputes by what His ears hear." I declare that this lifestyle will become a part of your daily inner drive.

To serve God acceptably, you must learn not to judge life situations by what your eyes see or what you have heard people say. Doing so brings you into a life of unrighteousness. The prophet said to God's people in Isaiah 8:13, "But the Lord of hosts, Him you shall hallow; Let Him be your fear, and let Him be your dread."

If there is anything in this world that should cause you to fear, it must be the power of God, to do what He desires or to even deny you heaven if you live a careless Christian life. Avoid the misuse of God's love for you. His love for you today is to help you live right before Him. At the end of all things, at the return of Jesus, God will not excuse your misuse of the salvation the blood of Jesus purchased for you, and the abundant grace provided.

Jesus said in Luke 12:4-5, "And I say to you, My friends, do not be afraid of those who kill the body, and after that have no more that they can do. But I will show you of whom you shall fear: Fear Him who, after He has killed, has power to cast into hell; yes, I say to you, fear Him!" Jesus was talking about the power of His Father.

What is the Fear of the Lord?

God wants you to seek grace to walk not only obedience to Him, but also walk in godly fear. The fear of God is not like being afraid that God is going to strike you down when you do wrong. The fear of the Lord begins with knowledge.

You may have just a little or an abundance of the knowledge of who God is. In addition, you may have a little or an abundance of knowledge of His expectations for your life—how to live and relate to the world and to people. If you seek the power of His grace to help apply this knowledge in your life to please God, you have the fear of the Lord. On the other hand, if you have the knowledge of God and His expectations for your life but you live to please self and fulfill the dictates of your ego, you have no fear of God.

Love Activates the Fear of the Lord

Your love for Jesus and your knowledge that He willingly shed His blood to redeem you must activate a strong love and an awesome regard for Him. Your love for God must translate into a life of obedience to His Word. It trains your heart to walk in the fear of God. Always remember, God gave Jesus for your redemption, so you would receive your new nature.

The writer of the book of Proverbs counsels you not to receive the Word of God in vain. You have to treasure it in your heart, just as you would silver. Then, you make your ears attentive to the wisdom it provides you, as you incline your heart to understand. Then you call out for insight and raise your voice to God for understanding. You search for the Word of God as you would for hidden treasures. Then, you will understand the fear of the Lord and find the knowledge of God (Proverbs 2:1-5).

To know God, you need Jesus Christ, who is the wisdom of God. If you walk in the fear of the Lord, Jesus will give you a measure of God's grace to help you know the ways of the Father. Knowledge of the Father will orient your life to please Him through a life of obedience.

LESSON: *Therefore, the fear of the Lord is to know a measure of God's nature and His requirement for your life—your lifestyle in this world, and in your interpersonal relationships. Then, you allow the knowledge you have to influence how you live, to His pleasure. Anyone, who has any level of knowledge of God and His requirement for his/her life but, live to please self, that one has no fear of the Lord.*

Grace and the Generation of the Last Adam

The old self is of the Adam generation, which is a rebellious and disobedient generation. The full measure of the Old Testament Law is past, but there is a twist, a new law is here for this new era of grace. This law is the law of the Spirit life in Christ Jesus. This is the law your life must learn to submit, as a Christian.

Anyone who submits to this law in Christ Jesus attains freedom from the law that rules the fallen nature—the Adam generation. It is the law of sin and death. This is not physical death. It is spiritual death. Spiritual death produces more death, which disables humans' ability to submit to God's Word and honor their creator in their life issues.

With the law of the Spirit of life working in you, and you live by the Spirit, it sets you free from condemnation (Romans 8:1). There is condemnation for all who live by the fleshly motivations, and consistently rejects God's Word.

If you are in Christ Jesus, and you honor Him through obedience, you receive the law of the Spirit of life, which helps you overcome the worldly craziness, motivated by the law of sin and death. You become a part of the Jesus generation of obedient people. These people are part of humanity, who love God, and who would choose death than to live unfaithful to God. This is the Spirit of Christ! It abides in all who consistently obey God, and in whom the Holy Spirit fully abides.

As you read earlier, Jesus is the head of all principalities and powers and dominions. In Jesus, you are complete and fashioned to overcome the world of disobedience. The presence of Christ in your life must produce His attributes—a life of obedience to God the Father. Your obedience to the Father will help you manifest the fruit of the Spirit. It is an indication Jesus, and the Father have come into residence in you.

LESSON: *One of the ways you can convince yourself you serve God, is when your life begins to manifest some of the attributes of Christ Jesus, which is your new nature or creation.*

LESSON: *Many of the self-motivated lifestyles and attitudes in this world reveal that, Jesus and the Father have not found a comfortable abiding place in people. Moreover, many do not fear the Lord.*

The Father was dwelling in Jesus to the full and He loved His Father. Jesus learned obedience to God, His Father. Consequently, He was full of the power of God's grace. He was bold to say to Satan, "Get behind me, Satan! For it is written, you shall worship the Lord your God and Him alone you shall worship".

LESSON: *If you serve the world, you get your needs met from Satan, who is the god of the world; but if you want to serve God, you depend on Him for all your needs, for He cares for you.*

The Bible calls on you to love the Lord your God with all your heart, and with all your soul, with your entire mind, and with all your strength. Jesus was in the world but not of it. The world did not have any influence on His life. Satan did not have the right to give Him anything His Father intended to give Him.

To love the Lord God, is to serve Him through obedience to His Word. God has blessed you with the nature of Jesus in your new self. The new self has the attributes of holiness, righteousness, and godliness. This is the Spirit of Christ, which must grow in your life if you belong to Jesus. The Bible says in Romans 8:9, "But you are not in the flesh but in the Spirit, if indeed the Spirit of God dwells in you. Now if anyone does not have the Spirit of Christ, he is not His."

Because you walk in obedience to God's Word, and practice the new nature in your life issues, that is, you workout your salvation, the grace of God activates the Spirit of Christ in you. This confirms you belong to Christ and He is in you.

LESSON: *The Spirit of Christ is the inner burning desire to do the will of God on a continuum, through obedience. This Spirit will motivate you, if you listen, to tell others about good news of God's favor in Jesus Christ.*

Because the spirit of Christ is at work in you, the spirit of excellence accompanies all the righteous things you put your hands to do. By the power of the grace of God, you will exhibit wisdom, knowledge, understanding, and power to make right judgments.

The Spirit of Christ will motivate, and enable you to walk in the fear of the Lord. It is therefore, very important to examine the things that motivate your daily life choices and decisions. If the Spirit of Christ works in you, the grace of God will work mightily in your daily life. It helps you to exhibit the fruit of the power of grace, which is victory over ungodliness and worldly lusts.

The Role Model

Jesus overcame the world because of His submission to the power of the Word of His God. God empowered Him to become a resource for the freedom of many (Acts 10:38). God anointed Him with the Holy Spirit, and with power. God has made Jesus the role model for your Christian life. God wants to empower you by the grace in Jesus Christ, to help you overcome the world as well.

LESSON: *Just as God anointed Jesus with the Holy Spirit and with power, Jesus want to anoint you with the Holy Spirit and with power to help you do all He has assigned to you fearlessly.*

Jesus said to you not to fear, because He has overcome the world. By Him, and by the grace you seek from Him, you can overcome the worldly enticements that could motivate you not to yield your all to the God who loves you.

Therefore, test if God's Word is what compels your lifestyle—in decisions, choices, even your thought processes. God has called you to walk in excellence just as your Savior.

LESSON: *True excellence in your life begins, when you learn to evaluate the things that go on in your environment by the Holy Spirit's voice in your inner self. You do not judge or evaluate life situations by what you hear from people or by what you see with your natural eyes.*

If you submit to the Lordship of Jesus, and to the voice of the Holy Spirit, the Spirit of Grace directs your life, and you bear fruit—the fruit of the Spirit. The fruit of the Spirit is an indication the Word of God, even Jesus, has a dominant place in your life. Refer to Galatians 5:22-25 for the fruit of the Spirit. Jesus demonstrated the effectiveness of living, and walking by the power of God's Word. He was full of

God's grace and He showed you how it is possible to live in this corrupt world, and overcome.

With the power of grace, you can overcome the craziness of evil and self-driven attitudes of this age, in order to submit to the will of God. In many instances, people, even some Christians, ignore God's requirement for their lives. This is so because they fail to acknowledge their identity in Christ, and its demand for obedience to God's Word. Consequently, they ignore the need to come to the throne of grace, to seek mercy and to find grace to help in their lives.

Chapter 11
The Grace of God and Transformation

The Bible says in Ephesians 1:3-4, that God, the Father of our Lord Jesus Christ, has blessed you with every spiritual blessing in the heavenly places, just as He chose you in Jesus before the foundation of the world. He did this to accomplish His goal in your life, that you should be holy and blameless before Him in love. Nevertheless, the greater things of God are not magical occurrences that fall in your lap.

The greater things of God's work in your life demand your cooperation through a life of obedience and diligence. God has predestined you for adoption as a son through Jesus Christ, according to His good pleasure. This is God's goal for your life, to conform you into the image of Jesus Christ, His Son.

God has made Jesus your role model. He wants you to learn from Jesus, to help you cooperate with Him in His conforming processes in your life. Therefore, your obedience to God has to approach that of Jesus as you mature in Him. Jesus obeyed God in entirety and God's fullness indwelled Him. Your ability to live in obedience will therefore accelerate your conformation, because the Father and Son come into residence in you.

LESSON: *As your obedience grows, God's fullness will grow also in your life. God's heavenly blessings will begin to manifest in your life in an increasing manner.*

Transformation and the Image of Christ

The Bible says in Romans 8:29, "For whom He foreknew, He also predestined to be conformed to the image of his Son, that He might be the firstborn among many brothers". In other words, God's goal is to create more people in the likeness of Jesus Christ, who would yield to Him through a life of obedience as Jesus did.

LESSON: *Examine your life to see if the obedience is growing in your responses in life. See if you honor God in your relationships with the world and with people.*

The Bible says in 2 Corinthians 13:5-6, "Examine yourselves as to whether you are in the faith. Test yourselves. Do you not know yourselves, that Jesus Christ is in you?—unless indeed you are disqualified. But I trust that you will know that you are not disqualified."

To help you discover if you are in the faith, verify if the Word of God is having influence in your life in today's corrupt and rebellious world. Check if the Word of God is what influences your decisions, choices, lifestyle, behavior, and your attitudes. To discover if Christ is in you, verify if at least the following are at work in your life:

- You are growing in the attributes of your new nature.
- You are growing in your manifestation of the yoke of Christ, which are meekness and lowliness. Jesus said in Matthew 11:29-30, "Take my yoke upon you and learn from me, for I am gentle and lowly in heart, and you will find rest for your souls. For my yoke is easy, and my burden is light."
- You are growing in your life of obedience to the Word of God.

Again, the Bible says in Philippians 4:5, "Let your gentleness be known to all men. The Lord is at hand." No matter your position in the secular world or in the church, God looks for humility and gentleness. This is so because He is in the process of conforming you to the image of His son, Jesus Christ. He wants you to learn to live with the yoke of Jesus—that submissive, and lowly attitude of the heart towards His voice (His Word). In addition, God wants to make His home in you (Isaiah 66:2).

LESSON: *Humility is an inner character. It is not an outward show. It is a heart issue. Jesus said He was gentle and lowly in His heart.*

LESSON: *To have rest for your soul implies you do not worry about what people say about you and you do not scheme to show people you are humble. To scheme, to show people your worth, takes you out of rest. Some will scheme moment-by-moment to keep up appearances.*

LESSON: *The Bible says God is transforming you into the image of His Son. That means, God is transforming you into that person who will live and practice His word in your life issues as Jesus did.*

Jesus lived and practiced the word of His Father. He said to the Jews, "When you have lift up the Son of Man, then you will know that I He, and that I do nothing of Myself, but as My Father has taught Me, I speak these things" (John 8:28). Your attitudes, behavior, thought processes must show that you are yielding to God's transformation.

Why the Image of Jesus Christ?

God is using the image of Jesus Christ, the Last Adam, as His solution for the failures and depravities among humans, the Adam generation. Unlike the first Adam, Jesus, the Last Adam, obeyed God completely. Hence, God wants to transform you and all of the redeemed into the image of Jesus Christ. In Jesus is the grace of God to help orient your life to cooperate with God's transformation processes.

Consequently, the grace of God through Jesus Christ is God's final solution, to help humanity orient herself to God's divine order—obedience to His voice (His Word), and to righteous and holy living. God desires holiness just as Jesus showed, when He said, "You shall be holy, for I am holy".

In his second letter to the believers, Apostle Peter wrote that the body of Christ waits for a new heaven and a new Earth, in which righteousness dwells. No wonder God wants you to grow in righteousness, which grows through a life of obedience to His Word.

The scepter of Christ's kingdom is righteousness (Hebrews 1:8). God commands you to practice the attributes of your new self in Christ Jesus. To accomplish this, Jesus has given to His church gifts, such as apostles, teachers, prophets, and evangelist, and pastors, for the building up of His people,

"Till we all come to the unity of the faith and to the knowledge of the Son of God, to a perfect man, to the measure of the stature of the fullness of Christ; that we should no longer be children, tossed to and fro and carried about with every wind of doctrine, by the trickery of men, in the cunning craftiness of deceitful plotting" (Ephesians 4:11-14).

Always remember you are no longer under the first Adam but the Last Adam, Jesus Christ. When you and the whole body of believers learn obedience, and attain to the fullness of Christ, God will have accomplished Romans 8:29 in the lives of His people of the church. Therefore, because you wait for these good things, the Bible encourages you to be diligent, so Jesus will come find you without spot or blemish, and at peace.

The Bible calls on you to feed on solid food, so you will come to full age. Solid food, the Word of righteousness, helps your conscience to come to greater level of understanding of God's purpose for your new life in Jesus Christ. It helps train your conscience to discern, and distinguish between good and evil, just as Jesus did.

The Bible encourages you to have the mind of Christ. This is why your mind has to be spiritual, by setting it on things above. That means your mind has to become Kingdom minded, and not worldly minded.

When you mature in Christ, you will learn not to judge life issues by what your eyes see or what your ears hear from others. You will learn only to judge life issues by the Holy Spirit, who is the Spirit of Truth. God wants you to seek His grace in Jesus to help you attain to this nature, the image of Christ.

LESSON: *To grow in righteousness is to grow in your obedience to the Word of God, and hence, it grows your life of holiness. You learn to allow the Word of God to have a dominant place in your life, and to influence your life issues.*

Apostle Paul said, "For in Christ Jesus neither circumcision nor uncircumcision avails anything, but a new creation. And as many as walk according to this rule, peace be on them, and mercy, and upon the

Israel of God". Heaven wants to see you walk, and manifest your new creation as the true a child of God He has made you.

The greater things of God that come to you requires a purposeful, and disciplined Christian life in your words, your thinking and your lifestyle, all of which the grace of God is here to help you orient to God's pleasure. Always remember that God is in the process of transforming you into the reality of who you are in His son, the image of Jesus Christ.

Therefore, the work of God in your life will eventually clothe you with the nature of Jesus Christ, who is the righteous and the holy One of God. These are the attributes of your new nature or new creation. God needs your cooperation in His transforming processes.

This places a demand on you to seek grace to help you learn obedience. Obedience purifies not only your soul, but it also enables your inner ears to hear your trainer, the Holy Spirit. Your obedience also fashions your mind to understand what the Holy Spirit says to you.

The Bible says in 1 Peter 1:22, "Having purified your souls by your obedience to the truth for a sincere brotherly love, love one another earnestly from a pure heart." Your life of obedience purifies your soul because obedience grows your righteous walk, which brings you into a state of holiness.

The Bible commands you to keep your heart with all vigilance, for from it flows your behaviors and attitudes in life issues. The issues of life proceed from the heart. You need the grace of God to learn to remain gentle, lowly, and submissive to God, which are powerful attributes of Jesus Christ, the Son of God.

As I indicated above, God has predestined you—His child, redeemed by the blood of Jesus—to be conformed into the image of Jesus His Son. Jesus bore the image of the invisible God, and God wants you to bear Jesus' image.

God, being the God of mysteries, has recreated a new you, and seated you with Jesus at God's right hand. God has hidden you with Christ in Himself (Colossians 3:1-3). To help you cooperate with God in your transformation, you need to acknowledge your current position in the heavenly places. Always see yourself as though you are a step to your maturity in God, to help keep you diligent in your pursuit of Christ.

King Nebuchadnezzar acknowledged the mysterious nature of God when he said to Daniel in Daniel 2:47, "Truly your God is the God of gods, the Lord of kings, and a revealer of secret, since you could reveal this secret". Again, the Bible says in Deuteronomy 29:29, "The secret things belong to the Lord our God, but the things that are revealed belong to us and to our children forever, that we may do all the words of this law".

No wonder Jesus said in Matthew 24:36, "But of that day and hour no one knows, not even the angels of heaven, but My Father only". Other Bible versions (ESV, ASV, ISV) add, "Nor the Son".

In Hebrews 1:3-6, the Bible says this: "Who being the brightness of His glory and the express image of His person, and upholding all things by the word of His power, when He had by Himself purged our sins, sat down on the right hand of the Majesty on high, having become so much better than the angels, as He has by inheritance obtained a more excellent name than they. For to which of the angels did He ever say: 'You are my Son, Today I have begotten You?' Again, 'I will be to Him a Father, and He shall be to Me a Son?' But when He again brings the firstborn into the world, He says: 'Let all the angels of God worship Him.' Praise God for His marvels!

Therefore, Jesus, the Word and the wisdom of God, came to the earth in human form but full of God Almighty, and in power. The will of God is that you will appropriate the power of God's grace to help you pursue, and become established in a life of love so God's fullness will indwell you also.

As your transformation approaches the image of Jesus the son of God, your behavior, your attitudes, and your relationships with people deviates from the ways of the world, and your thoughts become more kingdom oriented. Note that transformation cannot be complete in this life.

Transformation and Connecting to the Eternal

The Bible says in Ecclesiastes 3:11, "He has made everything beautiful in its time. Also, He has put eternity in their hearts, except that no one can find out the work that God does from the beginning to the end." God has put eternity in your heart. How can the eternity in you connect to the One who is eternal? To do so, you must know at least the following things:

1. Practice Your Identity In Christ

Know that you have an identity in Christ who is the image of the Eternal. Know your current position in the one who is eternal, the One who created your new identity—the Eternal has hidden you with Christ in Himself.

2. Live And Walk By The Spirit

The One who is eternal, is spirit, not a physical being. He gave you Jesus Christ, who took your sins on Himself in His physical body. He lived among us as the Son of the Eternal, but now seated with Him on His throne. If you live and walk by the Spirit of God in you, the law of the Spirit of life in Christ Jesus gives you the ability to avoid corruption that could retard your transformation, even your stand in Jesus Christ.

3. Know What You Have In Christ

The Eternal God has given to you His very great and precious promises (His Word) to live by. When you do, you escape corruption that is in the world, which comes by lusting after things that are outside of His will for your transformation. Because you escape corruption, you take on the divine nature of the Eternal.

Growing in the divine nature of the Eternal connects you to the Eternal. Jesus said your obedience to His Word would invite Him and the Eternal into residence in you. He said in John 14:23-24,"If anyone loves me, he will keep my word, and my Father will love him, and we will come to him and make our home with him. Whoever does not love me does not keep my words. And the word that you hear is not mine but the Father's who sent me."

LESSON: *Remember, God needs your cooperation in His transformation processes in your life. You cannot continue to live a fleshly life with a fleshly mentality and God just transforms you magically! God needs your cooperation!*

If God does not need your cooperation, He would have transformed all people in a second. However, because of His rewards, He identifies those who are willing versus the unwilling—people who have other priorities.

4. Practice Truth in Your Life

Because you have the grace of God, the Holy Spirit, and the attributes of a new nature, learn to pursue a life of truth. This is how you will learn from the Spirit of Truth, who guides and connects you to the Eternal.

5. Overcome Anxieties About Your Tomorrow

Jesus says to you not to be anxious about tomorrow. Remember Ecclesiastes 9:11, "Again I saw that under the sun the race is not to the swift, nor the battle to the strong, nor bread to the wise, nor riches to the intelligent, nor favor to those with knowledge, but time and chance happen to them all."

Do not be anxious about what your tomorrow holds for you. Just do the best you have the grace to do today, and leave tomorrow in the hands of your God. Refuse to misuse your today's opportunities!

LESSON: *Always remember that in many instances, the DNA of your tomorrow's successes is inherent in your today's opportunities!*

The Bible says in Ecclesiastes 9:10, "Whatever your hand finds to do, do it with your might, for there is no work or device or knowledge or wisdom in the grave where you are going". Again, the Bible says in Ecclesiastes 11:1, "Cast your bread on the waters; for you shall find it after many days." Therefore, do the best of the righteous things you have grace of God to do, as though there is no tomorrow.

6. Live and walk by Faith

Faith is to practice the Word of God you know. Because you believe God's Word, seek the grace of God to help you obey His Word in your choices and decisions in life. The above are some of the ways the eternity in you, will connect to the One who is Eternal.

Example of Satellites in Space

We have many satellites in the skies and we have systems and modules on Earth that can lock onto these satellites to receive and send information to far destinations. With these satellites and modules, many impossibilities of the past have become possible.

To harness the eternity within to help you lock onto the eternal and infinite God, you need the "module" called faith, and a renewed mind. The God who is transforming you is Spirit. Therefore, your mind must become spiritual or Kingdom minded to understand the God who is Spirit. Your faith makes the impossible, possible! In Christ, and by your faith, God wants your life to overcome the impossibilities He has ordained for your life, making them possible for you.

LESSON: *Because you have the Holy Spirit as your helper, seek grace to orient your life, your mind, and your heart to hear His voice in your spirit. He is the Spirit of God, who makes your desire to connect to the Eternal possible.*

LESSON: *If you have been a Christian for a while, seek grace to help you grow in the attributes of your new creation.*

It is important that you grow in the attributes of your new creation or new self, which helps you connect to the Eternal. Make it your sincere will to ask yourself, "What am I conforming to, and hence, what is my life transforming to?" This way you will catch yourself if you are conforming to the world or to Christ.

Remember that fleshly lifestyle denies you the ability to connect to the Eternal. As a redeemed individual, you have the liberty to yield to the conforming processes of the world, of self, or of God. You have the grace of God to yield to the conforming processes of God, to help you connect to Him who is Eternal.

Understand the delight, when you are able to connect to the Eternal. Your life becomes full and stable. You avoid the many evil ways of the world, which the law of sin and death motivates in people who do not have the Spirit of Christ.

Chapter 12
The Grace of God and the Power to Endure

Prophesying about the end time lifestyles, Jesus said in Matthew 24:10-13, "And then many will be offended, and will betray one another, and will hate one another. Then many false prophets will rise up and deceive many. And because lawlessness will abound, the love of many will grow cold. But he who endures to the end shall be saved."

Endurance is to keep on with the righteous life or things you do without wavering in the face of opposition and challenges. Jesus is saying to all that, in the midst of the challenges this world presents to you, you have to endure and overcome. That way, your love for Jesus and your obedience to Him will grow.

The world presents to you the lifestyle of lawlessness, with all its betrayals, disingenuous love, and hatred among people. However, you have the grace of God to help you endure through all and overcome. With the grace of God, you can remain unscratched spiritually.

Among others, lawlessness and challenges in life come to do some things in your life. Therefore, stay awake, watch and guard the following:

- Life situations will either improve your view of life, making you increasingly kingdom minded (which helps you avoid corruption in the world), or it will corrupt you if you allow them in your life.
- They test your stability in Jesus Christ, or the roots you have built into Him. They will reveal your willingness to endure and overcome lawlessness and challenges.
- If you handle the lawlessness and challenges incorrectly, it could deny you the ability to pursue the life God requires out of your redeemed life in Christ Jesus. God expects your life to display

righteousness, holiness, and godliness, all in the truths of God's Word before the eyes of the world.

Daily yield to Christ and the things that happen to you will turn out for your good. Though lawlessness and challenges in life are your enemies, they also serve as spiritual conditioning for your life in Christ Jesus. It must re-orient your mind for consistent Kingdom mindedness.

Therefore, the Bible says in Hebrews 10:36-39, "For you have need of endurance, so that after you have done the will of God, you may receive what is promised. For, "Yet a little while, and He who is coming one will come and will not tarry. Now the just shall live by faith; but if anyone draws back, my soul has no pleasure in him. But we are not of those who draw back to perdition, but of those who believe to the saving of the soul."

Enduring the Test of Faith

Your faith will preserve you to the end, even in the midst of lawlessness and selfish inclinations among people in this life. God's power will do this for you because you always seek grace to live faithful to Him. God tests your faith for genuineness. Your genuine faith will make you stand strong and overcome whatever the world will throw at you and all the fiery darts of the devil. How do you make your faith genuine? You do so by adding what the Bible commands you in 2 Peter 1:5-7.

You need to learn endurance! For this reason, you need as much of God's grace as you can get. The Bible counsels you not to fall short of the grace of God. Failure to fortify yourself with the grace of God could make you bitter due to life issues. Bitterness also could creep into your heart, due to perceived offenses from people.

The Bible encourages you in Romans 5:2-5, "Through whom also we have obtained access by faith into this grace in which we stand, and we rejoice in hope of the glory of God. More than that, we rejoice in our sufferings, knowing that suffering produces endurance, and endurance produces character, and character produces hope, and hope does not put us to shame, because God's love has been poured into our hearts through the Holy Spirit who has been given to us."

LESSON: *If you fail to endure all the world throws at you, heaven will see you as double-minded, and unstable in all your ways. If you learn to endure, especially in times of temptation, heaven will approve you for the crown of life.*

You are blessed if learn to endure and overcome the evils of this age. God wants you to learn endurance, because that is how you will prove your love for God, and you know that He exists, and will reward you for enduring in your diligent pursuit of Him.

God has called you to endure, and stand firm against the maneuvers of the devil. To do so, God wants you to ensure yourself that He is your Father, and He will supply all your needs. This way, you will deny anxiety from taking a piece of your heart. Then, you can live with a sober mind, which helps you live a vigilant life as a child of God.

Your ability to stand firm is how the God of all grace will perfect, establish, strengthen, and settle you (1 Peter 5:7-10). You have to seek the grace of God to help you stand firm to the end of any difficulty you may be going through. This is how you will do the will of God to obtain His promises for you.

LESSON: *The devil is after the Word you have gained in Christ! God always has some spiritual and material blessing for you after your endurance. The devil desires that you will lose what God has for you. These are the things that could enrich and make you strong in Jesus Christ.*

Chapter 13
Receiving the Grace of God in Vain

It is very important to understand that the grace of God is not a covering, which permits you to continue in a lifestyle that deviates from God's expectations for your new life in Jesus Christ. Rather, the grace of God is here to help you live like a champion in this world, overcoming the things that diminished the Adam generation, and which denied them the ability to do what pleases God.

The covering you have is the blood of Jesus, which activates God's mercy, even though for now, your lifestyle deviates from God's expectations. Understand that you have the opportunity to yield to the power of God's grace while you are alive.

If you claim to have the grace of God, you are saying you have submitted your life to the Word, the wisdom, and the power of God, which Jesus Christ represents. Because you have grace, God expects you to increasingly grow in your victory over ungodliness and worldly lusts. He expresses His patience towards you through Jesus Christ, His son. These lifestyles bring corruption in your life if you allow them. The grace of God is the source of your triumph in this world.

LESSON: *Corruption is worldly pursuits, which takes you out of God's purpose for your redeemed life. It opens you up for worldly lifestyles and mindsets that introduce blemishes in your life of righteousness, holiness, and godliness.*

God wants you to take advantage of His grace to help you overcome all that the world will throw at you, even the unseen enemies of God who would come against you in this life. The Bible says you can do all things through Christ who strengthens you. This is so because the grace and truth came through Jesus to help you to triumph over the world.

LESSON: *If you yield your life to the Word, the wisdom, and the power of God in Jesus Christ, you will do yourself extremely good.*

The Fullness of Grace Available to you

The grace of God has appeared to all humanity. This is so because Jesus Christ came into the world for all people. When you receive Jesus, you come into the fullness of God's grace. In Christ, you know God has called you to come to the throne of grace. There, you obtain mercy and find grace to help you in your times of need. The grace of God is the Word that gives you direction, the wisdom to help you know what to do, and the power of God you need to accomplish what heaven demands of you in this life as you live through Jesus Christ. It helps you overcome in this life. Anyone that submits to the Holy Spirit receives the enabling power, the wisdom, and Word of direction to overcome life evils.

LESSON: *If you claim to be under grace and your life appears to easily yield to ungodliness and worldly lust, you may have received the grace of God in vain.*

Apostle Paul's question in the book of Romans is therefore very appropriate. He asked in Romans 6:1, **"**What shall we say then? Are we to continue in sin that grace may abound?" He answered this question, "By no means!" The reason is that, in your baptism, God aligned you with the death of Jesus Christ. Therefore, God expects you to acknowledge your old self as dead and hence, everything about your old attitudes, lifestyles, mindsets, and behavior, have now become your enemies. The Bible encourages you not to practice your old self because that nature died with Christ, and must not still influence your new life.

You must therefore, acknowledge that grace is not a license that permits or excuses you to practice your old attitudes and evil ways. Acknowledge you are not the same person you were before Christ. Death took place in your baptism and you must acknowledge your old self as dead and not your friend any longer. Death must mean death!

The Bible says to you in Ephesians 4:22, "That you put off concerning your former conduct, the old man which grows corrupt according to the deceitful lusts".

For many of us Christians, it takes a long time to come to this conclusion. Note that during the years of slavery, slaves changed hands. One master would purchase a slave from another. If a new master purchased a slave, the slave and his family would belong to the new master. Concerning this matter, the blood of Jesus has purchased you and His Church. Therefore, everything about your life belongs to Jesus Christ. Apostle Paul had a revelation about this truth. He wrote in 2 Corinthians 5:14-15, "For the love of Christ compels us, because we judge thus: that if One died for all, then all have died, and He died for all, that those who live should no longer live for themselves but for Him who died for them and rose again."

Also, understand that the transaction for your new status comes with repentance. Repentance must precede baptism, which makes your baptism genuine, and a very powerful spiritual experience. It represents death to certify that you now belong to a new master, Jesus Christ. This is how the Holy Spirit empowers you to will and walk in your newness of life. The Bible says in Romans 6:4, "Therefore, we were buried with Him through baptism into death, that just as Christ was raised from the dead by the glory of the Father, even so we also should walk in newness of life."

The grace of God comes with the power of the Holy Spirit, who is the Spirit of Grace, to help you overcome your inabilities. This is so because the grace of God comes to you through Jesus Christ.

Today is the day of God's abundant mercy and favor. He has expressed His softer side through Jesus Christ. If you die, all you have done in this life remains sealed until the Day of Judgment, "As it is appointed for men to die once, but after this the judgment" (Hebrews 9:27). As long as you live in this life, you have all the grace of God available to you to help you make adjustments in your life and to align your life to the requirements of God.

LESSON: *If you claim to be under grace, in a state of grace, or have received grace, heaven must see you as one who is overcoming ungodliness and worldly lusts. You are indeed overcoming your old ways of living. In* *fact, Heaven want you to overcome the life and lifestyle that denied you the power of the new nature in Christ.*

Grace is not a covering over your misbehaviors and wicked lifestyle. The grace of God does not permit you to live contrary to God's Word. Rather, because you are in Christ and under grace, your life must show that the Word of God is changing you. Jesus, the Word, the wisdom, and the power of God, became flesh and dwelt among us. Through Him came these attributes of God to help you conquer just as He did. If there is no indication that you are overcoming in this life, you may have received the grace of God in vain.

God gave His law through Moses. Unfortunately, the children of Israel could not keep the law. Grace is not like the law. Grace has come through Jesus not only to do what the law did for the children of Isreal, but more. The law pointed out the wrongdoing of the children of Israel but lacked the power they needed to overcome.

The grace that has come through Jesus Christ, not only points out our wrongdoing through the Word and by the Holy Spirit, but also provides the wisdom, the power, and truth to overcome wrongdoing. This is one of the things, which differentiate the law from the grace of God. Through Jesus Christ, God makes available to you all the grace you need to help you overcome in this age of corruption, self-motivations, and lawlessness.

Therefore, as I stated earlier, if you claim to be under grace, there must be evidence of an increasing triumph in your life over ungodliness, worldly lust, and over the inward and outward display of evil, which lacks truth. These things captivate people who do not have the life of Christ.

Grace of God and Victory over Ungodliness

God has imputed to you a new nature to help you manifest His glory in this world, wherever He places you. The attributes of this new nature include godliness. Understand that though you have received the new birth and the godly nature from God, you are not completely walking in it yet. Therefore, God commands you to put on your new nature, which is the new man. That means God wants you to practice godliness in your life issues—in your choices, decisions, and in your relationships.

As you practice who you are in Christ, the attributes of your new self (or new nature) grow and provide you victory over ungodliness.

LESSON: *Ungodliness comes from your behaviors and deeds that deviate from the godly nature God has imputed or ascribed to your new self in Jesus Christ.*

Ungodliness is a wicked and immoral lifestyle. It is a wicked and immoral lifestyle because it ignores the Word of God and hence, the call to holiness. Bad behavior corrupts your spirit and your life deviates from holiness. Obedience cleanses you from an immoral life of lawlessness— from the life that fails to yield to God's Word. God has all grace for you to do what He expects of you. He calls on you to separate yourself from the ways of the world because He wants to live in your life.

Judgment against Ungodliness

God is holy and He says to you in 1 Peter 1:16, "You shall be holy, for I am holy." Moreover, 2 Corinthians 7:1, says "Therefore, having these promises, beloved, let us cleanse ourselves from all filthiness of flesh and spirit, perfecting holiness in the fear of God." By the fear of God, you avoid the evil ways of this age. Without the fear of God, it is impossible to avoid ungodliness. God wants you to cleanse not only your body, but your spirit as well.

The Bible says in Jude 1:14-15, "Behold, the Lord comes with ten thousands of His saints, to execute judgment on all, to convict all who are ungodly among them of all their ungodly deeds which they have committed in an ungodly way, and of all the harsh things which ungodly sinners have spoken against Him."

Ungodliness must not continue to be a part of your lifestyle because you have received the grace of God and a godly new nature. Rather, you must learn to live as a person who is going to be part of the soon-coming judges—the saints of Jesus! You are the redeemed and God wants you in heaven unless you have given up on your faith and trust in your Redeemer.

The Mind and Ungodliness

Ungodliness will take advantage over you if your mind is not renewing. Your mind must continually renew and become progressively Kingdom oriented. This is how you can overcome fleshly thinking and fleshly, ungodly deeds. You do this with God's grace in Jesus Christ, which you must seek. It is impossible to do this apart from the grace of God.

The Bible described some of the children of Israel as idolaters. They allowed the world around them to define their behavior. They became gluttonous, drunkards, and some indulged in sexual immorality. Consequently, twenty-three thousand of them failed to reach the land of promise. They were destroyed in a single day in the wilderness. What is the lesson you must learn?

LESSON: *Take heed to your life so you do not allow the world around you to influence how you live your Christian life.*

In Galatians 5:19-21, the Bible shows you the works of the flesh, which could deny you heaven. It says this: Now the works of the flesh are evident: sexual immorality, impurity, sensuality, idolatry, sorcery, enmity, strife, jealousy, fits of anger, rivalries, dissensions, divisions, envy, drunkenness, orgies, and things like these. It warns that if you allow these lifestyles in your life, you will not inherit the kingdom of heaven.

LESSON: *Therefore, it is important not to confuse your life that yields to Galatians 5:19-21 with the desire to inherit the kingdom of heaven. If you let the lifestyle described in Galatians five overtake your life, you are denying yourself the opportunity to inherit heaven.*

The Bible cautions you to take heed, and not think you are all right or to think you stand, least you fall. No matter where you are as a Christians or the number of years you have been a Christian, you have to take heed to self-satisfaction. Self-satisfaction can open doors to carelessness in your life, which could get you to fall. The Christian life or the upward call is a daily pressing forward and deeper into Christ where you can find protection against a fall.

Apostle Peter commands you in 2 Peter 1:5-10 to add some qualities to your faith, without which your life would become unfruitful and vulnerable to a fall.

We know that Apostle Paul was a mature, tenacious Christian. Nevertheless, he said in Philippians 3:12-14, "Not that I have already attained, or am already perfected; but I press on, that I may lay hold of that for which Christ Jesus has also laid hold of me. Brethren, I do not count myself to have apprehended; but one thing I do, forgetting those things which are behind and reaching forward to those things which are ahead, I press toward the goal for the prize of the upward call of God in Christ Jesus."

LESSON: *If you are maturing in your Christian life, you aught to learn to forget your past hurts. Rather, set your eyes, and crave for the things Jesus Christ has set before you. Focusing on your past hurts could slow down God's transformation in your life.*

Any Christian that is mature or maturing must grow in Apostle Paul's way of thinking, even to grow to have the mind of Christ.

LESSON: *Remember that in life, there are more opportunities before you than in your past. Therefore, do not let your past draw you into ungodly thinking.*

Remember, Jesus endured many things in this life for God to perfect Him, and He became the source of your eternal salvation. Jesus said that He had the opportunity to sit with His Father on His throne because He, Jesus, overcame the world. He wants you to overcome the world with His grace so you will sit with Him on His throne.

Do not let the life of ungodliness become the reason you fail to press towards realizing your identity in Christ and your heavenly calling. The Bible says there is a cloud of witnesses all around you, including those in the spiritual realm, cheering you on and desiring that you learn to endure and overcome ungodliness, sin, and the weights that are all around you. They desire, and want you to make it to heaven. Look for things set before you, and learn to pursue life as Jesus did.

You have to regard the Christian calling as a journey upward, towards heaven. Therefore, you learn to avoid lifestyles and behaviors that becomes "spiritual baggage". Do not allow them attach themselves to your life, and you learn to endure through many difficulties and challenges. Even then, because you love God, you will always come out on top, because of His promises in Romans 8:28 and 1 Corinthians 10:13. All you have to do in your difficult seasons is to stay still through prayer, declaring His promises back to Him, and you will know that your Savior Jesus is Lord.

LESSON: *To become an idolater does not necessarily mean you set up alter to a spiritual being to worship. You can create idols in your heart! Whenever you exalt anything in your heart above your devotion to God, you have an idol.*

Acknowledge that God the Father has called you to share a measure of Christ's glory. Therefore, do not build "castles" for your glory in this world. They will become idols in your mind, and will share your devotion to God. If you build these idols, they will only become subject to the fires of Christ. He will tear down at the day of His appearing.

The above paragraphs have points you have to take note. The truth is that, there are certain Christians who could miss the purpose of God's grace for lack of understanding. Consequently, they could fail to acknowledge that the grace of God is not here to do what God expects from your redeemed life, but grace provides you the ability to fulfill God's expectations. If you fail to acknowledge this truth, your life could yield to idolatry, and hence, could put Christ to the test in your ignorance.

In addition, because you are the righteous of the Lord who have received grace from Jesus, God wants you to understand the things that could confront you in this life. In Psalm 34:19-20, the Bible makes you aware that, "Many are the afflictions of the righteous, but the Lord delivers him out of them all. He guards all his bones; not one of them is broken." Be encouraged, and learn to endure all the afflictions that could come in your life, because you know the Lord's coming could be soon. Gird up your mind, be sober, and set your heart on the grace that is coming to you when Jesus returns.

LESSON: *Your ungodly behavior, attitudes and mindsets enslaves you. They become your master because they overcome you. Whatever overcomes a person, to that he is enslaved.*

The Grace of God and Behavior

Is your behavior and character changing because you have received the grace of God? The Bible encourages you in Hebrews 12:15-16, "Looking carefully lest anyone fall short of the grace of God; lest any root of bitterness springing up cause trouble, and by this many become defiled; lest there be any fornicator or profane person like Esau, who for one morsel of food sold his birthright". Unlike Esau, do not allow bad behaviors and today's worldly pleasures cause you to miss your inheritance in heaven.

Because bitterness has "roots", it defiles not only you, but others as well. Do not become the source of the bitterness that defiles many others. Understand that after salvation, your life heads for your inheritance in heaven. How you live after salvation will determine whether you will possess your inheritance or not. Therefore, your lifestyle, and behavior after salvation are very important in your responses to the heavenly call— your inheritance in heaven.

LESSON: *Do not be like Esau, who had the inheritance set before him but allowed his today's cravings for fleshly desire to cause him to miss his inheritance. You have grace to endure to the end.*

LESSON: *Bitterness in your heart defiles you and it takes you out of holiness, which is a requirement for heaven.*

The will of God for you is your sanctification (consecration). There are behaviors, and lifestyle in the world that corrupt your soul. That is one of the reasons God commands you to cleanse your body and spirit from all things that defile. To become defiled takes you out of consecration or holiness.

LESSON: *Bitterness comes in two ways. You can have bitterness towards people who have not treated you well or bitterness could proceed out of your heart towards people you envy. Neither of these ways is acceptable to the Lord for your redeemed life.*

The Bible brings your attention to the behavior of the children of Israel in their journey from the Red Sea to the land of promise. The Bible says they were all under the cloud and they passed through the sea. They all ate the same spiritual food, manna. They drank the same spiritual drink from the Rock that followed them. The Rock was Christ. Nevertheless, with most of them God was not pleased, for they were overthrown in the wilderness.

Why did they suffer that fate at the hands of the God who delivered them from bondage? The reason was their behavior! Why do you have to be concerned about the life of the children of Israel, which happened centuries ago? The Bible says in 1 Corinthians 10:11-12, "Now all these things happened to them as example, and they were written for our admonition, upon whom the ends of the ages have come."

It is therefore very important not to take the battle against your fleshly and worldly motivations lightly. You must always resist these motivations with the grace of God, and prevent them from taking your lifestyle into things that do not edify you as a Christian. Apostle Paul punished his body to keep his lifestyle and behavior under check, "But I discipline my body and bring it into subjection, lest, when I have preached to others, I myself should become disqualified".

LESSON: *Note that your financial successes are not a measure of your good character. Rather, the product of your behavior measures your character.*

Grace and the Yoke of Jesus

Jesus wants your attitudes towards people, and your responses to life to convert, and become like a child. This is Jesus' way of communicating to you the need to humble your heart, to help you enter the kingdom of heaven. In the journey to the kingdom of heaven, you do not prove to anyone your worth, no matter who you are in life or in church. You do not prove you are the boss of your life because the grace of God has produced, and has made you who you are.

Therefore, God wants you to pursue life with humility of heart. God says to you in Micah 6:8 that He requires you to do what is just, pursue mercy towards others, and to walk humbly before Him. If you are not a person redeemed by the blood of Jesus, and you are a person in the world, your responses to life could be different. However, because you have received the power of the grace of God, He expects your responses to life, and your lifestyle to be one of humility.

LESSON: *Understand that your life displays your attitude, and intents before the God who is everywhere, even though you do not see Him.*

God wants your approach to life, and your attitudes and responses in this world to differ from people in darkness. Then, you become the light of Christ wherever God places you. Jesus says your humility is one of the doorways to the kingdom of heaven, and into your greatness.

If your burden in this life is heavy and it prevents you from doing God's will, go to Jesus to seek His grace. His grace will train your heart to deny pride, so you can take on His yoke. His yoke is His gentleness and lowness of heart.

LESSON: *You sometimes are not able to do the will of God in your Christian life because of where your heart lives. Other times, because your heart, not entirely yielded to Jesus, pose challenges when confronted with the call to do God's will.*

The meekness and lowliness of Jesus is the recipe for a good heart, which you need to help you to obey the Word of God. Gentleness helps you to grow in self-control. Then, your attitude in life becomes sustainable. You will not be up one day and down the next, because someone offends you. If Jesus had no self-control, He would have fallen into the traps of the devil, who tried to get Jesus to sin just one time.

Grace to Avoid Tempting Christ

The Bible encourages you not to put Christ to the test, as some of the children of Israel did in their journey to the land of promise. Consequently, serpents destroyed some of them. There are "serpents" in this life. When a serpent bites you, it releases its poisonous venom into your body, which begins to work against the function or wellness of your body. As the serpent did to Eve in the Garden of Eden, these serpents could encourage deeds, lifestyles, mindsets, and attitudes that deviate from who you are in Christ. These lifestyles and behaviors can work against your spiritual health if you allow them into your life.

What does it mean to test Christ? Do you remember the temptation Jesus went through in the wilderness at the hands of Satan? Satan said to Jesus in Matthew 4:6, "If you are the Son of God, throw yourself down. For it is written: 'He shall give His angels charge over you, and in their hands they shall bear you up, Least you dash your foot against a stone.'"

What was Jesus' response? Jesus said to Satan, "It is written again, 'You shall not tempt the Lord your God'". To tempt, is to lay a snare or to lure in an attempt to cause another to fail or deceived. Learn not to test Christ!

LESSON: *Fortify yourself with God's grace to deny Satan's ability to motivate you to pursue deeds and behaviors that test Christ.*

How do you Tempt Christ

You may know God's promise concerning your life situation. However, do not allow Satan to lie to you, and trick you into obeying his command, to arrogantly yield to applying the promise of God outside of His divine order. If you do this to show you have faith, you test Christ.

It is true that the angels of God would bear up Jesus if He threw Himself down, because that was God's sure promise. However, because Jesus was in close communion with His Father, He did not allow Satan to cause Him to do what God was not telling Him to do at that moment. Moreover, if Jesus had jumped, He would be obeying Satan's suggestion and hence, would become a slave of Satan just like the rest of humanity, whom He came to save.

The Bible says in Romans 6:16, "Do you not know that to whom you present yourself slaves to obey, you are that one's slaves whom you obey …" If you allow your flesh or any spirit to motivate your actions or deeds to show you have faith, you become a slave of your flesh or that spirit. This way, you test Christ!

LESSON: *Motivations of the flesh take you out of God's pleasure because those who yield to the motivations of the flesh cannot please God.*

LESSON: *If, for the sake of advantage, you yield to Satan's suggestions in your difficult times, you are ignorantly yielding your life to slavery in some areas, and you test Christ.*

LESSON: *As a Christian, who has abundance of grace your calling is to live for Jesus and obey Him. However, if you live to please self and you question God's ability to take care of you it is equivalent to tempting Christ.*

Grace to Overcome Grumbling

Another behavior of the children of Israel in their journey to their land of promise, was grumbling. The Bible encourages you not to grumble, as some of them did, and destroyed by the destroyer. The Bible says in Philippians 2:14-15, "Do all things without grumbling or disputing, that you may become blameless, innocent children of God without fault in the midst of a crooked and perverse generation, among whom you shine as lights in the world."

God has promised to direct your life by His Holy Spirit, so you will learn to do His will. Since you have the call of God on your life, He wants you to produce fruit of His Spirit. The fruit includes love, joy, peace, long-suffering, kindness, goodness, faith, meekness, and self-control. These qualities in your life act as a law. It is the law of the Spirit of life in Jesus Christ, which helps you triumph or sets you free from the law that draws fallen humanity into ungodliness and worldly lusts. The law of the Spirit of life in Jesus keeps you at rest in your God, and out of grumbling.

In your rest in God, you are able to establish your heart on Christ. Consequently, He enables you by the power of His grace to live with the awareness of His soon coming. The knowledge of Christ's soon coming is able to motivate your sincere life of faith, helping you to avoid ungodliness, and to purify your life (1 John 3:1-3).

LESSON: *If you are a Christian and your life is Christ-centered, you receive the ability to deny ungodliness and worldly lusts because you know Christ is coming soon.*

If you are a Christ-centered Christian, you learn to grow out of grumbling about God's work in your life. You learn not to gossip about others. When you grumble, you question God's work in your life—you question His management of your life, and you tell God He is not doing a good job in managing your life.

Apostle James wrote to believers in James 5:8-9, "You also be patient. Establish your hearts, for the coming of the Lord is at hand. Do not grumble against one another, brethren, lest you be condemned. Behold, the Judge is standing at the door."

LESSON: *If you are a Christian who grumbles, and questions God's work in your life, you are likely to yield to offenses by others.*

Grace to Overcome Worldliness

Drunkenness is associated with spiritual carelessness. A careless Christian is spiritually drunk with worldly ways, and not motivated by the Holy Spirit, the Spirit of Grace. Christ has provided you with His grace to help you stand strong in your faith. The lack of self-control leads to a life that is subject to carelessness, which opens you up for many worldly lifestyles to attach to your life. Consequently, your lifestyle could deviate from the pleasure of Christ because you become worldly!

Apostle Paul narrated what he endured in order to stay out of worldliness. He said in 2 Corinthians 6:4-10 that he endured the following as the servant of God:

- Much patience, tribulations, needs, distresses, stripes,
- Imprisonments, tumults, labors, sleeplessness, fasting,
- Purity, knowledge, long-suffering, kindness, the Holy Spirit,
- Sincere love, the Word of Truth, the power of God,
- Weapons of righteousness on the right hand and on the left,
- Glory and dishonor, evil report and good report,
- Regarded as a deceiver and yet true,
- As unknown, and yet well known,
- As dying, and yet he lived, as chastened, and yet not killed,
- As sorrowful, yet always rejoicing, as poor, yet made many rich,
- As having nothing yet possessing all things, all things because, his Jesus possesses all things.

Worldliness and Your Blessings

In Genesis 13, Abraham took on himself Lot, his nephew. Abraham was very prosperous. After a while, Lot also became prosperous, and there was strife between the herdsmen of Abraham and of Lot. Therefore, Abraham said to Lot, "Let there be no strife between you and me, and between your herdsmen and my herdsmen, for we are kinsmen. Is not the whole land before you? Separate yourself from me. If you take the left hand, then I will go to the right, or if you take the right hand, then I will go to the left".

At Abraham's words, Lot chose for himself all the ancient Jordan Valley, and Lot journeyed east. Thus, they separated from each other.

LESSON: *When pride comes in your heart because of your material wellness, you could ignore courtesy. Lot, who had favor from Abraham, would not insist that Abraham make his choice first.*

LESSON: *If you know whom you belong, and your identity in Christ, you do not scramble for worldly things as the people of the world would. Abraham was calm, and did not scramble to choose the best area for himself.*

It was after they went their both ways that the Lord said to Abraham, "Lift up your eyes and look from the place where you are, northward and southward and eastward and westward, for all the land that you see I will give to you and to your offspring forever. I will make your offspring as the dust of the earth, so that if one can count the dust of the earth".

LESSON: *What is it in your life that stands in the way of God's blessings for you? Is it worldliness? Is it worldly mindset? Let worldliness go, let "Lot" go! God will proclaim His blessings on your life if you let go ungodliness.*

If you are experiencing lack in your life, in your today, consider it from both the spiritual and physical point of view, just as Apostle Paul. God has subjected all things to Jesus, and He can supply all your needs if you ask Him.

LESSON: *If you fail or refuse to endure the things the world throws at you, and overcome them, your life could yield to worldliness.*

Grace of God— a Great Teacher

The Bible refers to the grace of God as a teacher, who teaches you. The grace of God has come to assist, and teach you to live a life that is pleasing to the Father. The grace of God is not here to help you excuse yourself of any ungodly lifestyle in this world. Rather, grace is the power God provides through Christ, to help and train you to do the will of God. You can only do the will of God with the help of His grace.

Jesus said in John 15:5-6, "I am the vine; you are the branches. He who abides in me and I in him, bears much fruit; for without me you can do nothing. If anyone does not abide in me, he is cast out as a branch and is withered; and they gather them and throw them into the fire, and they are burned."

Without Jesus, you can do nothing, because in Him is found the power, the wisdom, and the Word that helps you do God's expectations in entirety for your redeemed life. Without the grace of God, you have no teacher and you will be subject to attitudes, behaviors, and ways of the world.

Because the grace of God is a teacher, you have to learn to make yourself a good student. It is possible to have the best teacher in the world, but if you do not learn, He will not profit you. Remember, the Holy Spirit is the Spirit of Grace, who is here to guide you into many things of the truth, for the benefit of your new life in Jesus Christ.

If you fail to obtain God's grace, it is an indication you have failed to respond to the command to go to the throne of grace. If that happens in your life, the Bible compares you with Esau. Esau had the inheritance set before him—the inheritance that had come down from Abraham to his father Isaac. Unfortunately, Esau had other priorities in life, and diminished the importance, and the enormity of the inheritance (birthright). He valued his cravings for his fleshly satisfaction more than the inheritance due him.

One day, Jacob boiled soup and as Esau came from the field, he was faint. Esau said to Jacob, "I beg you, Let me eat of the red, this red soup, for I am faint". Jacob told Esau to sell his birthright in exchange for the red soup. Then Esau said, "Behold, I am at the point of dying, and what profit shall this birthright be to me?"

Jacob asked Esau to swear to the transaction between them, and Esau did. He swore and sold his birthright to Jacob. Upon Esau swearing, Jacob gave him bread and the soup. Esau ate and drank, rose up, and went his way. The Bible says Esau despised his birthright (recorded in Genesis 25:29-34).

LESSON: *The grace of God teaches you to be diligent in the pursuit of your inheritance in Jesus Christ. It teaches you to respond correctly to Apostle Peter's call in 2 Peter 1: 10, "Therefore, brethren, be even more diligent to make your calling and election sure, for if you do these things you will never stumble."*

For the abundance of grace God has given, you do not have to "sell" your inheritance reserved for you in heaven, for the fleeting pleasures of this world. Let God's grace help you to deny ungodliness and worldly lusts. Perceive your inheritance in heaven as precious, and something worth dying to attain. You must die to your fleshly cravings, which diminish your strength in Jesus Christ.

LESSON: *Do not let what God allows in your life cause you to sell your inheritance. Nothing that you go through in today's world, which God permits, will deny you His promises. Oftentimes, God uses your situations to tests your hunger for your inheritance reserved for you in heaven, and other times, your resolve to obey Him.*

The test God takes you through grows your faith. He wants your faith to grow in genuineness. By your faith, God keeps you to your inheritance. In addition, your genuine faith overcomes the world, and anything the world throws in your way. Genuine faith will overcome the fleshly cravings of today's world.

The Grace of God and the Inner Drive

Very often, you may desire to please God while overcoming life issues. Unfortunately, the inner drive could remain un-yielded to Jesus Christ. Therefore, there is contention between the power of your inner drive and the grace of God, which could prevent you from receiving from God (refer James 1:5-8).

Consequently, unlike the children of Israel and the law, you have abundance of the grace of God to examine, and test yourself to verify where your inner drive lives. Failure to do so could make the grace of God powerless in your life, though it is not without power to do what God intended it to do.

This is one of the reasons you could receive the grace of God in vain. Let the love of Christ for you motivate you to yield your total life to Him. Have confidence that He cares about your life more than you do for yourself. That way, you will yield your all to Him.

LESSON: *Understand that any area of your life not yielded to Christ will eventually come back to give you problems.*

Chapter 14
Growing in the Grace of God

"But grow in the grace and knowledge of our Lord and Savior Jesus Christ. To Him be the glory both now and forever. Amen." — 2 Peter 3:18.

To grow in the grace of God begins with your life of obedience to His Word. The life of obedience activates in you the spirit of wisdom to help you know God. Growing in the grace of God also produces strength in you, which activates many abilities in your life. God commands you to find grace to serve Him acceptably through reverence and godly fear.

As I indicated earlier, to reverence God is to obey Him, His Word. Therefore, one area of walking in the strength of the grace of God is to grow in your obedience to God. Since God is invisible, to walk in the strength of God is to grow consistently in obedience to His Word. God's goal is to bring His submitted children to the full stature of the measure of Jesus' obedience to Him. Jesus was the first person in human form who obeyed God completely.

There are greater levels of obedience to God, which results in the manifestation of His power through you. This is so because the Father and Son come into residence in you. In addition, to become strong in the grace of God is to grow in the fear of the Lord. It is important to realize that, you will mature in holiness because you submit to the life of the fear of the Lord.

By the fear of the Lord, you will depart from evil and life issues that present the potential of corruption in your life. The lack of the fear of the Lord is the cause of many lifestyles, attitudes, behaviors, and thought processes that deviate from the standards set for the redeemed of the Lord.

The grace of God provides the ability to reject ungodliness and worldly lusts that takes captive the people who walk in darkness. To serve God acceptably is to grow in the power of grace. If you are growing in your ability to reject ungodliness, and worldly lusts, it is an indication you are growing strong in grace.

LESSON: *You can claim to be under grace; however, if you are not growing in your ability to reject ungodliness and worldly lusts, your claim has no foundation or spiritual validity or strength.*

Worldly lust always, opens doors for corruption to gain access into your life all over again. If corruption gains access into your life, it works to diminish the significance of your identity in Christ. It also diminishes the progress of your spiritual transformation into the image of Jesus Christ.

God has a solution for those who submit to Him. The Bible says God's solution is the provision of His exceedingly great and precious promises. The people, who learn to define their daily life issues by the word and promises of God, will receive the power of grace to overcome the corruption that is in the world. The result is their ability to grow in the godly attribute of their new creation. Therefore, they participate in the divine nature of God, which always overcomes corruption.

God calls on you to find grace to help you. Your education, social status, or religious status cannot help you. The only force that can help you is the grace He has provided for you in Jesus Christ. That is why apart from Jesus, you can do nothing.

LESSON: *To grow in the grace of God, you must grow in the attributes that make up the grace of God—the Word, wisdom, and the power of God.*

Growing in Wisdom

In respect to gaining or growing in wisdom, Apostle Paul prayed for the believers in Ephesians 1:17, "That the God of our Lord Jesus Christ, the Father of glory, may give you the spirit of wisdom and of revelation in the knowledge of Him." Therefore, to grow in wisdom is Jesus enlarging His presence in your life because He is the wisdom of God.

The Bible says this about Jesus in Isaiah 11:2, "The Spirit of the Lord shall rest upon Him, the Spirit of wisdom, and understanding, the Spirit of counsel and might, the Spirit of knowledge and the fear of the Lord". If you have Jesus, and you live a submitted life to Him, you will grow in not only wisdom, but also understanding, counsel, might, knowledge, and the fear of the Lord.

The fear of the Lord allows you to grow in wisdom. It is therefore important not to take the fear of the Lord lightly in your Christian life. After salvation, your life steers you toward your Promised Land, which is the kingdom of heaven. Therefore, you need more wisdom correctly to handle your life issues to God's pleasure.

LESSON: *The fear of the Lord is a dynamic force that enables you to avoid the evil ways. It also grows you in wisdom. Lack of the fear of the Lord is the result of many ungodly attitudes and behaviors among God's people all over the world.*

These benefits come into your life, because you learn to obey the Word of God. The Bible says, "For the Lord gives wisdom; from His mouth come knowledge and understanding; He stores up sound wisdom for the upright; He is a shield to those who walk in upright; He guards the paths of justice, and preserves the way of His saints. Then you will understand righteousness and justice, and Equity and every good path. When wisdom enters your heart and knowledge is pleasant to your soul" (Proverbs 2:6-10).

Because you take the Word of God seriously, the knowledge it provides becomes pleasant to your soul. Discretion will preserve you; understanding will keep you, to deliver you from the way of evil.

Growing in the Power of God

Growing in the grace of God is also to grow in the power of God, which Jesus represents. Jesus said you would receive power when the Holy Spirit comes upon you. Consequently, to grow in the power of grace is to grow in the power of the presence of the Holy Spirit in your daily life. The way you do this is a daily pursuit of the attributes of your new creation, which is holiness, righteousness, and godliness. You do not want to engage in lifestyles that diminish the presence of the Holy Spirit in your life.

If God has imputed to you the attributes of Christ, learn to practice these attributes in your life decisions, choices, lifestyle, and in all you do. This is how your life will take on the divine power of God. The power of God in you is the "resurrection" power—the power that resurrected Jesus from the dead. This power exceeds any power that could tear you down from your faithfulness to the Lord Jesus.

Regarding growing in the power of God, you have to heed Apostle Paul's word in Galatians 5 and 6. In Galatians 5:6, he said, "For in Christ Jesus neither circumcision nor uncircumcision avails anything, but faith working through love." In addition, in Galatians 6:15, he said, "For in Christ Jesus neither circumcision nor uncircumcision avails anything, but a new creation."

The greatest thing you can do in your Christian life is to find grace to obey God's command, to put on the attributes of your new creation. This is how the power of God will become evident in your life and ministry, including all you do through faith and love. If you are rooted and established in your love for God and for people, you will comprehend the dimensions of Christ's love for dying on the cross for you. Consequently, God establishes Himself in you—His fullness.

LESSON: *To grow in the power of God, you must discipline your life with the attributes of your new nature in Christ Jesus, because that is the source of your power. The Holy Spirit does not empower careless and lawless children of God.*

Growing in the Knowledge of the Word

Growing in the grace of God is also to grow in the knowledge of the Word of God. As I indicated in chapter 10, the Bible counsels you to let the Word of Christ dwell in you richly in all wisdom, teaching and admonishing one another in psalms, hymns, and spiritual songs, singing with thankfulness in your hearts to the Lord (Colossians 3:16). Learn to do whatever you do to God's glory.

Whenever you obey this command, you do yourself much good. If you enrich yourself with the Word of Christ, the Word will counsel you and teach you in the ways you should go. The Bible says faith comes by hearing and hearing by the Word of God. The Word of God has a voice, which will speak to your spirit, if you are the one who loves to feed yourself with the Word daily.

Consequently, if you are rich in the Word of Christ, the Holy Spirit will instruct you by the Word. When God said He would instruct and teach you in the way you should go, He does this by His Spirit and by His Word. Therefore, grow in grace by growing your knowledge of the Word of God. In Proverbs 2:4, the Bible encourages you to seek the Word of God as you would money in this world, and search for it as you would treasures of this world.

Growing in the Word of God stabilizes your life, because it is your source of confidence in this turbulent world of deception, evil, and selfish motivations. Growing rich in the Word of Christ, makes you into a vessel the Lord can use to counsel others in their difficult times.

LESSON: *The effective ways to become productive with the Word of Christ is to learn to practice or live by the Word. You do not grow strong in your Christian life by having the word in your "head" only.*

If you practice the Word of Christ in your life, it will grow you in wisdom, and you will understand the fear of the Lord. It will help you understand righteousness, justice, equity, and every good path in this life. Therefore, you must not take the call to grow in grace lightly.

What is the conclusion?

Once again, I want to stress, and very important to understand that the grace of God is not a covering, that permits you to live anyhow. It is not a covering, that permit you to continue the lifestyles and behaviors, which deviates from God's expectations for your redeemed life in the Lord. The grace of God is His final solution for the inconsistent lifestyle of the Adam generation. It helps bring the Adam generation come to Jesus to receive salvation, and the power to live a triumphant life in this corrupt world. Therefore, do not receive the grace of God in vain. Use grace to triumph in this world, and to please God.

The Bible says in Hebrews 10:29-30, "Of how much worse punishment, do you suppose, will he be thought worthy who has trampled the Son of God underfoot, counted the blood of the covenant by which he was sanctified a common thing, and insulted the Spirit of grace? For we know Him who said, "Vengeance is Mine, I will repay", says the Lord. Again, "The Lord shall judge His people.""

Therefore, do not receive the grace of God in vain. Rather, use the grace of God to produce fruit in your Christian life, triumphing over ungodliness, worldly lusts, which could lead you into lawlessness.

In conclusion to this book, "The Power of God's Grace: The final Solution", I encourage you to live faithful to Jesus. Do not allow all that goes on in the world cause you to live unfaithful to Jesus for two reasons:

- You attain to your eternal salvation if you live faithful to Jesus through obedience, just as Jesus to His Father.
- You are encouraged to "Be sober, be vigilant; because your adversary the devil walks about like a roaring lion, seeking whom he may devour. Resist him, steadfast in the faith, knowing that the same sufferings are experienced by your brotherhood in the world. But may the God of all grace, who called us to His eternal glory by Christ Jesus, after you have suffered a while, perfect, establish, strengthen, and settle you. To Him be the glory and the dominion forever and ever. Amen" (1 Peter 5:8-11).

Knowing the above promise from God, you have to learn endurance in your Christian life, so you will do the will of God, and gain the promises. As I said earlier, your life in Christ is on God's watch and He cares about everything in your life.

Concluding Prayer

Dear Father, in the name of Jesus Christ, your holy Son, I bring myself under subjection to you. Remove anything in my life that stands in the way of my closeness to you, and your presence in my life. Let the power of your grace in Jesus Christ help me with strength and power, to stand strong as the redeemed of the Lord. Deliver me from any bondage, spiritually, physically or emotionally, to help make the grace powerful in my life. Help me live like a champion in this corrupt world, over evils and self-motivations. Help me yield my all to you and make me into a vessel in your hands to help others.

Author Contact:

WorthyLamb Ministries International
Website: http://www.worthylambtech.com
YouTube: Search for "good08God"
Email: worthylambministry@sbcglobal.net

Printed in the United States
By Bookmasters